THIS BOOK HAS BEEN
DONATED TO THE POULTNEY
HIGH SCHOOL THROUGH
GREEN MOUNTAIN COLLEGE
AND THE VERMONT CAMPUS
COMPACT PARTNERSHIP
GRANT FOR 2005-2006

GENE THERAPY

THE newbiology

GENE THERAPY

Treating Disease by Repairing Genes

Joseph Panno, Ph.D.

Facts On File, Inc.

GENE THERAPY: Treating Disease by Repairing Genes

Copyright © 2005 by Joseph Panno, Ph.D.

Facts On File, Inc.
132 West 31st Street
New York NY 10001

Library of Congress Cataloging-in-Publication Data

Panno, Joseph.
 Gene Therapy : treating disease by repairing genes / Joseph Panno.
   p. cm. — (The "new biology" series)
 Includes bibliographical references and index.
 ISBN 0-8160-4948-3 (alk. paper)
 1. Gene therapy. I. Title.
 RB155.8.P36 2004
 615.8'952003025851

Facts On File books are available at special discounts when purchased in bulk quantities for businesses, associations, institutions, or sales promotions. Please call our Special Sales Department in New York at (212) 967-8800 or (800) 322-8755.

You can find Facts On File on the World Wide Web at http://www.factsonfile.com

Text design by Erika K. Arroyo
Cover design by Kelly Parr
Illustrations by Richard Garratt and Joseph Panno

Printed in the United States of America

MP FOF 10 9 8 7 6 5 4 3

This book is printed on acid-free paper.

For my wife, Diana,
who worked with me in the lab for many years,
and for my daughter Eleanor,
who knew about cells before she could read or write.

⚬✕⚬

CONTENTS

⚭

Preface   xi

Acknowledgments   xiii

Introduction   xv

1   *Genetic Disorders*   *1*

Immune Deficiencies   1

Breast Cancer   4

Colon Cancer   5

Melanoma   5

Cystic Fibrosis   6

Hemophilia   7

Liver Disease   9

Cardiovascular Disease   10

Muscular Dystrophy   11

Alzheimer's Disease   11

Parkinson's Disease   12

Huntington's Disease   13

2   *Viruses: The Cornerstone of Gene Therapy*   *14*

Viruses Are Living Crystals   15

Viral Genomes May Be RNA or DNA   16

Viruses Evolved from Plasmids   22

Viruses Know How to Infect Cells   23

The Virus as a Gene Vehicle   28

Viruses Used in Gene Therapy   29

3 Ashi DeSilva: A Promising Start   **32**

Clinical Trials Defined   34

Cells of the Immune System   35

Adenosine Deaminase (ADA)   38

Preliminary Research   40

Clinical Procedure for ADA Gene Therapy   42

The DeSilva Clinical Trial   42

4 Jesse Gelsinger: Down to Earth   **45**

Ornithine Transcarbamylase (OTC)   46

Preliminary Research   48

Clinical Procedure for OTC Gene Therapy   49

The Gelsinger Clinical Trial   51

The Investigation   52

Concluding Remarks   54

5 Future Prospects   **56**

Safer Vehicles   56

Reducing Immune Rejection of the Vector   61

Improved Risk Assessment   63

Redesigning Human Anatomy and Physiology   65

6 Ethics of Gene Therapy   **71**

The Belmont Report   71

Clinical Trials   74

Physiological Enhancement   76

Cosmetic Applications   77

7 Legal Issues   **79**

Regulatory Agencies   80

The Gelsinger Legal Trial   83

International Regulation   86

8 Resource Center   **87**

Eukaryote Cell Primer   87

Recombinant DNA Primer   107
The Human Genome Project   118
X-Linked Severe Combined Immunodeficiency
    (SCID-X1)   121
Alzheimer's Disease (AD)   123
Huntingdon's Disease (HD)   124

Glossary   125
Further Reading   151
Index   157

PREFACE

Ꚉ

The New Biology set consists of the following six volumes: *The Cell, Animal Cloning, Stem Cell Research, Gene Therapy, Cancer,* and *Aging.* The set is intended primarily for middle and high school students, but it is also appropriate for first-year university students and the general public. In writing this set, I have tried to balance the need for a comprehensive presentation of the material, covering many complex fields, against the danger of burying—and thereby losing—young students under a mountain of detail. Thus the use of lengthy discussions and professional jargon has been kept to a minimum, and every attempt has been made to ensure that this be done without sacrificing the important elements of each topic. A large number of drawings are provided throughout the series to illustrate the subject matter.

The term *new biology* was coined in the 1970s with the introduction of recombinant DNA technology (or biotechnology). At that time, biology was largely a descriptive science in danger of going adrift. Microbiologists at the turn of the century had found cures for a few diseases, and biologists in the 1960s had cracked the genetic code, but there was still no way to study the function of a gene or the cell as a whole. Biotechnology changed all that, and scientists of the period referred to it as the new technique or the new biology. However, since that time it has become clear that the advent of biotechnology was only the first step toward a new biology, a biology that now includes nuclear transfer technology (animal cloning), gene therapy, and stem cell therapy. All these technologies are covered in the six volumes of this set.

The cell is at the very heart of the new biology and thus figures prominently in this book series. Biotechnology was specifically designed for studying cells, and using those techniques, scientists gained insights into cell structure and function that came with unprecedented detail. As knowledge of the cell grew, the second wave of technologies—animal cloning, stem cell therapy, and gene therapy—began to appear throughout the 1980s and 1990s. The technologies and therapies of the new biology are now being used to treat a wide variety of medical disorders, and someday they may be used to repair a damaged heart, a severed spinal cord, and perhaps even reverse the aging process. These procedures are also being used to enhance food crops and the physical characteristics of dairy cows and to create genetically modified sheep that produce important pharmaceuticals. The last application alone could save millions of lives every year.

While the technologies of the new biology have produced some wonderful results, some of the procedures are very controversial. The ability to clone an animal or genetically engineer a plant raises a host of ethical questions and environmental concerns. Is a cloned animal a freak that we are creating for our entertainment, or is there a valid medical reason for producing such animals? Should we clone ourselves, or use the technology to re-create a loved one? Is the use of human embryonic stem cells to save a patient dying from leukemia a form of high-tech cannibalism? These and many other questions are discussed throughout the series.

The New Biology set is laid out in a specific order, indicated previously, that reflects the natural progression of the discipline. That is, knowledge of the cell came first, followed by animal cloning, stem cell therapy, and gene therapy. These technologies were then used to expand our knowledge of, and develop therapies for, cancer and aging. Although it is recommended that *The Cell* be read first, this is not essential. Volumes 2 through 6 contain extensive background material, located in the final chapter, on the cell and other new biology topics. Consequently, the reader may read the set in the order he or she prefers.

ACKNOWLEDGMENTS

I would first like to thank my friend and mentor, the late Dr. Karun Nair, for helping me understand some of the intricacies of the biological world and for encouraging me to seek that knowledge by looking beyond the narrow confines of any one discipline. The clarity and accuracy of the initial manuscript for this book was greatly improved by reviews and comments from Diana Dowsley and Michael Panno, and later by Frank Darmstadt, Executive Editor; Dorothy Cummings, Project Editor; and Anthony Sacramone, Copy Editor. I am also indebted to Ray Spangenburg, Kit Moser, Sharon O'Brien, and Diana Dowsley for their help in locating photographs for the New Biology set. Finally, I would like to thank my wife and daughter, to whom this book is dedicated, for the support and encouragement that all writers need and are eternally grateful for.

INTRODUCTION

When we get sick it often is due to invading microbes that destroy or damage cells and organs in our body. Cholera, smallpox, measles, diphtheria, AIDS, and the common cold are all examples of what we call an infectious disease. If we catch any of these diseases, our physician may prescribe a drug that will, in some cases, remove the microbe from our bodies, thus curing the disease.

Unfortunately, most of the diseases that we fall prey to are not of the infectious kind. In such cases, there are no microbes to fight, no drugs to apply. Instead, we are faced with a far more difficult problem, for this type of disease is an ailment of our genes. Since the 1990s, scientists have identified several thousand genetic disorders that are known to be responsible for diseases and conditions such as cancer, senility, diabetes, and asthma. Gene therapy attempts to cure these diseases by replacing the damaged gene that is causing the problem.

Although there are thousands of genetic defects that could, in principle, be treated with gene therapy, only a small percentage are considered practical candidates for this type of treatment. Diseases that qualify for gene therapy are debilitating disorders that affect more than 1 percent of the population, the conventional treatments for which are ineffective, costly, or difficult to administer. Many people opt for gene therapy simply because it is their best chance for a normal life, even if they are not completely cured. Gene therapy is a new, potentially dangerous procedure and thus requires careful attention to the selection process. Consequently, all clinical trials are carefully screened and monitored by government granting agencies. For example, trials conducted in the United States are regulated by the Food and Drug Administration (FDA) and the National Institutes of Health (NIH), while trials in the United Kingdom are controlled by the Gene Therapy Advisory Committee, established by the Department of Health.

The first gene therapy trial, conducted in 1991, was designed to treat an immune system disorder known as adenosine deaminase (ADA) deficiency. ADA weakens the immune response so that the individuals suffering from this disorder are unable to fight off even mild infections. There were only two patients in that trial, one of whom showed a modest recovery, while the second patient, a young girl named Ashi DeSilva, showed a dramatic improvement. This trial proved to the research community that gene therapy could work. Many other gene therapy trials were launched throughout the 1990s, but none of them lived up to their expectations. Indeed, a trial conducted at the University of Pennsylvania in 1998 ended in disaster when one of the patients, a young man named Jesse Gelsinger, died as a direct result of the treatment. The consequences of this trial were profound as they affected not only gene therapy but also all experimental therapies that involve human subjects. Critics at the time pointed out that gene therapy should not be called a therapy at all, but an experimental procedure, a status that it retains to this day.

Since the birth of recombinant DNA technology, in the early 1970s, scientists have dreamed of using their new "tool kit" to cure genetic diseases, and now it appears that dream may come true. But the fulfillment of that dream is producing a therapy that is extremely hazardous and surprisingly difficult to apply. The complicating element of the therapy is reliance on a virus to carry the therapeutic gene into the patient's cells. Generally, the virus, known as a vector, is injected into the bloodstream, where it comes into contact with cells of the immune system. The immune system destroys most of the vector particles before they can enter the appropriate cells, thus abolishing much of the therapeutic effect. When the vector gains access to some of the cells the immune system treats this like any other infection and tries to kill the cells harboring the vector. The immune system attack on the infected cells has two consequences: The immune system kills the cells containing the vector, thus further minimizing any therapeutic effect or, if the number of cells harboring the vector is very high, the immune system will damage or destroy whole organs in an attempt to rid the body of the vector, with potentially fatal consequences for the patient. Despite these very substantial problems, the number of disorders being treated with gene therapy has increased from a few in 1990 to more than 600 in 2004, and of all the technologies provided by the new biology, gene therapy holds the promise of unlimited potential for curing disease and reversing the effects of age.

This book, another volume in the New Biology set, discusses the science behind gene therapy, as well as the ethical and legal issues associated with this therapy. Earlier chapters describe genetic diseases that may be treated with this therapy and the viruses that are used to deliver therapeutic genes to the cell. These discussions are followed by two case studies: the first involves Ashi DeSilva, the first patient ever treated with this therapy, and the second profiles the case of Jesse Gelsinger. The future prospects of gene therapy are examined from the perspective of its one great success (DeSilva) and its greatest failure (Gelsinger). Two chapters are devoted to the ethical and legal debate surrounding this powerful, but often dangerous therapy. The final chapter provides background material on cell biology, recombinant DNA technology, and other topics that are relevant to gene therapy.

.1.

GENETIC DISORDERS

When a gene is damaged, it usually is caused by a point mutation, a change that affects a single nucleotide. Sickle-cell anemia, a disease affecting red blood cells, was the first genetic disorder of this kind to be described. The mutation occurs in a gene that codes for the beta chain of hemoglobin, converting the codon GAG to GTG and resulting in a protein that has the amino acid valine at position 6, instead of glutamic acid. It may seem like an insignificant difference, but this single amino-acid substitution is enough to cripple the hemoglobin molecule, making it impossible for it to carry enough oxygen to meet the demands of a normal adult.

Sickle-cell anemia, like many genetic disorders, is monogenic, being caused by a single defective gene. But many forms of cancer and some neurological disorders are polygenic, involving several mutated genes. The genetic disorders described in this chapter are of both kinds and are being treated in clinical trials, or will be in the near future. Taken together, these diseases account for more than 200,000 deaths in North America each year. Although the range of ailments treatable with gene therapy is extremely broad, more than 65 percent of the clinical trials are aimed at curing various forms of cancer.

Immune Deficiencies

All animals have an immune system that is designed to combat invading microbes, and without it, we face certain death from a multitude of diseases. Our immune system consists of an enormous population of white blood cells that appear in many different forms, the most impor-

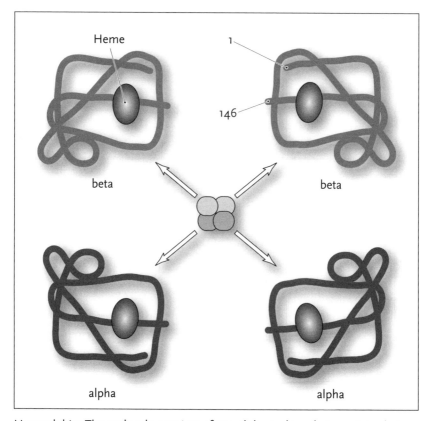

Hemoglobin. The molecule consists of two alpha and two beta protein chains, each bound to an iron-containing heme group that carries oxygen. The position of the first (1) and last amino acid (146) is indicated. Ancestral hemoglobin probably consisted of a single alpha or beta chain.

tant of which are the B cells, T cells, and macrophages. B and T cells are lymphocytes that develop in bone marrow and the thymus, respectively. Macrophages are phagocytic blood cells—they confront invaders head-on by eating them—whereas B cells attack foreign material indirectly by producing antibodies. T cells control and coordinate the immune response by releasing signaling molecules called cytokines that recruit macrophages and B cells. T cells also have the remarkable ability to detect invaders that are hiding inside a cell. Even more remarkable, they can force the infected cell to commit suicide in order to control the spread of the infection.

A common form of immune deficiency is severe combined immunodeficiency-X1 (SCID-X1). This disease represents a group of rare, sometimes fatal, disorders that destroy the immune response. Without special precautions, the patients die during their first year of life. Those who survive are susceptible to repeated bouts of pneumonia, meningitis, and chicken pox.

All forms of SCID are inherited, with as many as half of the cases being linked to the X chromosome. The mother passes on this disease, since males born with this disorder usually die before reaching their reproductive years. SCID-X1 results from a mutation that cripples a receptor for a cytokine called interleukin 2 (the IL2R gene). The IL2R protein activates an important signaling molecule called Janus kinase 3 (JAK3). A mutation in the JAK3 gene, located on chromosome 19, can result in a second form of SCID. Defective cytokine receptors, and the signaling pathways they activate, prevent the normal development of T lymphocytes that play a key role in identifying invading agents, as well as activating other members of the immune system.

A third form of SCID is due to a mutation in the adenosine deaminase (ADA) gene, located on chromosome 20. This gene is active in T lymphocytes and the mutation leads to a toxic buildup of adenosine inside the cell, thus blocking the normal maturation and activity of this crucial member of the immune system. Some patients suffering from ADA deficiency can mount a weak immune response, but in most cases the response is abolished. The conventional treatment, involving a bone marrow transplant, has been successful in saving many lives, but acquiring a compatible tissue match for every patient is extremely difficult and sometimes impossible.

In many ways, SCID is an ideal candidate for gene therapy since the T cells can be collected from the patient and grown in culture, where the healthy gene is inserted and tested. If the T cells take up the gene and express it properly, they can then be injected into the bloodstream of the patient. It is for this reason that the very first gene therapy trial (profiled in chapter 3) involved a young patient suffering from ADA deficiency. That trial was a success, and a recent trial, involving SCID-X1, has reported complete success in curing this form of immune deficiency.

Breast Cancer

Breast cancer, like all cancers, is a genetic disorder caused by a mutation in one or more genes. Viruses cause some cancers, but the mechanism still involves a corruption of genetic information equivalent to a naturally occurring mutation.

Breast cancer is the second most common cause of cancer death in women around the world, with an estimated 50,000 deaths per year in the United States alone. Two genes, BRCA1 (breast cancer 1), located on chromosome 17, and BRCA2, on chromosome 13, were isolated in 1994. Mutations in either of these genes are associated with the occurrence of

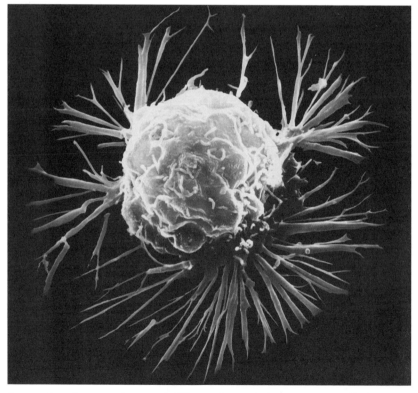

A scanning electron micrograph (SEM) of a single breast cancer cell, showing its uneven surface and cytoplasmic projections. Breast cancer is the most common cause of cancer in women. Magnification unknown. *(SPL/Photo Researchers, Inc.)*

breast cancer and ovarian cancer. The proteins produced by these genes are involved in repairing damage to DNA, and their loss can lead to a buildup of errors in DNA replication that can lead to cancerous growth.

General screening of the population for BRCA1 and BRCA2 is not yet recommended, but several clinical gene therapy trials are under way that are attempting to replace or supplement the mutated genes with normal copies. Some of the trials are also attempting to introduce tumor-suppressor genes into breast cells to block development of the cancerous growth.

Colon Cancer

Colon cancer strikes more than 100,000 people every year in North America, resulting in more than 50,000 deaths. Actively dividing cells, such as those that line the colon, are especially prone to cancer development because of errors that can occur when DNA is replicated. Environmental factors, such as diet and cigarette smoke, play a role, but two genes have been identified that can make an individual especially susceptible. One of these genes, called MSH2, is located on chromosome 2, and the second, MLH1, is on chromosome 3. Patients carrying mutations in either of these genes are typically diagnosed with colon cancer before the age of 50. MLH1 and MSH2 code for proteins that are involved in postreplicative mismatch repair of DNA. The loss of these repair enzymes leads to a genomewide accumulation of multiple point mutations, favoring cancer development. Several gene therapy trials are under way.

Melanoma

Every year, more than 40,000 people in North America alone are diagnosed with melanoma, the most aggressive form of skin cancer, and of those diagnosed, nearly 8,500 will die from this disease. Melanoma is often initiated by overexposure to sunlight, and although remission under treatment is common, the risk of recurrence is very high.

A mutation in a gene on chromosome 9, known as cyclin-dependent kinase N2 (CDKN2), makes the carrier more susceptible to this form of cancer. CDKN2 codes for a protein called p16 that is an important reg-

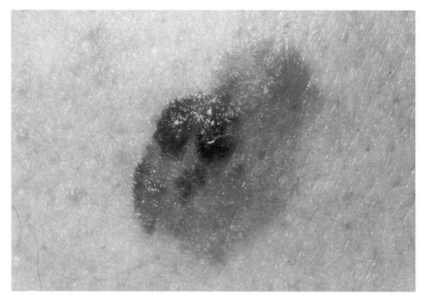

A close-up of the skin of a 71-year-old man showing the growth of a malignant melanoma (darkest area). Melanomas are a common form of cancer that is being treated in gene therapy clinical trials. *(SPL/Photo Researchers, Inc.)*

ulator of the cell division cycle, in particular, the timing of DNA synthesis. A defective p16 allows uncontrolled cell division, which is a common characteristic of cancer cells. Uncontrolled proliferation of the skin is usually apparent with the appearance of dark, irregular-shaped moles, appearing on the nose, forehead, and upper torso.

Prevention is the first strategy against this cancer, by using protective clothing and sunscreen. Conventional treatments involve surgical removal of the tumors and radiation therapy. Several gene therapy trials are under way with the aim of replacing or supplementing the mutated p16 gene with a normal copy. In addition, some trials are attempting to introduce nonspecific antitumor genes that will stimulate the immune system to destroy tumor cells.

Cystic Fibrosis

Of all the genetic diseases, cystic fibrosis (CF) is the most debilitating. This disease is associated with the production of thick, sticky mucus that clogs the lungs, making breathing difficult and providing an environment that is susceptible to bacterial infection. Indeed, most sufferers of CF die of congestive lung failure, brought on by a bacterial infection, before age 30.

CF is caused by a mutation in a gene that codes for a sodium chloride transporter, called CFTR, found on the surface of the epithelial cells that line the lungs and other organs. Several hundred mutations have been found in this gene, all of which result in defective transport of sodium and chloride by epithelial cells. The transporter can tolerate some amino acid substitutions, so the severity of the disease varies depending on the site of the mutation. The most common mutation does not cripple the transporter, but it does alter its three-dimensional shape, and as a consequence, the sorting machinery in the Golgi complex never delivers it to the cell membrane. (The eukaryote cell and the function of the Golgi complex are described in chapter 8).

The loss of the CF transporter reduces the amount of water on the cell surface, thus increasing both the density of the mucus layer and the acidity inside the cell. The abnormal acid level leads to the production of a defective glycocalyx that is unable to repel bacteria; as a consequence, a specific bacterium, *Pseudomonas aeruginosa,* is free to infect and destroy lung tissue. Conventional treatments are available that thin the mucus layer and kill *Pseudomonas,* but they are only partially successful. Patients suffering from CF must undergo regular treatment to dislodge the mucus in order to clear the airways, and for them, life is a daily battle against suffocation.

The CFTR gene was cloned in 1990 and shown to be located on chromosome 7. Many gene therapy trials are under way, and because CF is a monogenic disorder, hopes are high that a cure will be possible very soon.

Hemophilia

A remarkable thing happens whenever we cut ourselves: Some of our blood, which is normally a liquid, is converted to a fibrous solid at the site of the wound. The blood clot so formed has several functions: It reduces blood loss, it covers the wound to prevent bacterial infection, and it provides a temporary patch until the cells repair the damage. The formation of a blood clot is a complex process that involves at least a dozen enzymes and protein factors. The principal elements in the clotting process are the proteins prothrombin, thrombin, and fibrinogen. These proteins are modified in sequence, with the help of several clotting factors, to produce fibrin, the protein from which clots are made.

Hemophilia A is a disease characterized by a failure of the clotting process. It is caused by a mutation in the clotting factor VIII gene

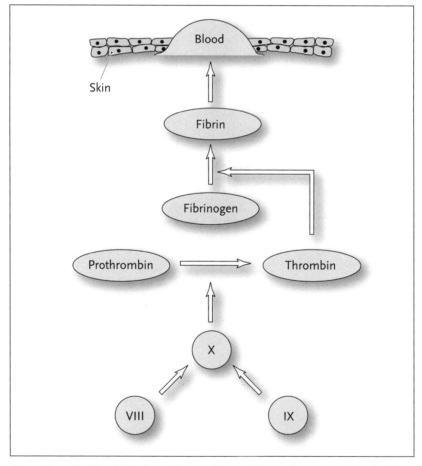

Formation of a blood clot. Two clotting factors (VIII and IX) activate a third (X) which stimulates conversion of prothrombin to thrombin. Thrombin then catalyzes the conversion of fibrinogen to fibrin to convert the drop of blood collecting at a wound to a solid clot.

(*hema*), located on the X chromosome, affecting one in 5,000 males. A second and much rarer form of this disease, (Hemophilia B), is due to the loss of clotting factor IX. Hemophilia B is sometimes called Christmas disease after Stephen Christmas, the first patient to be diagnosed with this form of hemophilia, and for a time, factor IX was called the Christmas factor. The chromosomal location of the factor IX gene is unknown. Both clotting factors, VIII and IX, are synthesized in the liver.

A famous carrier of Hemophilia A was Queen Victoria, who transmitted it through the birth and marriage of her many children to the royal families of Germany, Spain, and Russia. Males are susceptible to this disease because they have only one X chromosome. Females, with two X chromosomes, are not likely to have a defective *hema* gene on both chromosomes and so rarely show the symptoms of this disease.

Conventional treatment of Hemophilia A has involved regular transfusions of normal blood to replace the defective clotting factor, but this was a major inconvenience and often led to liver damage. Contamination of human blood supplies with the AIDS virus, and the resulting infection of many hemophiliacs in the 1980s, forced the development of alternate sources of factor VIII for replacement therapy, including antibody-purified factors and the production of factor VIII using DNA recombinant technology. These procedures produce safe, high-quality clotting factors but are extremely expensive.

Gene therapy trials involving factor VIII gene transfer to liver and bone marrow cells in experimental animals have not resulted in sustained production of the clotting factor. A recent attempt to introduce the gene into gut epithelia appears to be more successful and may soon lead to human clinical trials. Gene therapy trials involving factor IX have been more successful, and we may see a cure for this form of hemophilia in the near future.

Liver Disease

Proteins that we eat for food are broken down (catabolized) to amino acids, which may be used to generate energy or to construct proteins for our own use. A major by-product in the catabolism of amino acids is ammonia, the stuff of Earth's ancient atmosphere and a molecule that in high concentrations is toxic. Cells deal with the toxicity by converting the ammonia to urea, a much safer molecule that passes out of our bodies as urine. The production of urea depends on the liver enzyme ornithine transcarbamylase (OTC). If OTC is defective, blood levels of ammonia increase rapidly, resulting in coma, brain damage, and death.

The gene for OTC has been isolated and localized to the X chromosome. Accordingly, liver disease, like hemophilia, affects males but rarely females. Some males show a partial deficiency in OTC due to somatic cell mosaicism; that is, some of the liver cells produce the normal enzyme. Traditional treatment involves a rigid diet and constant monitoring of blood ammonia levels. But this approach has been only partially effective, and it often leads to repeated comas, each of which carries a 15 percent risk of mortality or brain damage. Because OTC is expressed exclusively in the liver, where general detoxification of the blood occurs, liver transplants have been attempted, but with little success.

Being monogenic, with a single organ affected, liver disease is an ideal candidate for gene therapy. However, a clinical trial in 1999 designed to cure this disease (profiled in chapter 4) ended in disaster, bringing all other trials to a halt for more than a year. Further trials are now under way with a new set of guidelines and protocols, and expectations are high that gene therapy will be able to cure liver disease in the near future.

Cardiovascular Disease

Atherosclerosis is a disease of the arteries that can strike at any age, although it is not a serious threat until people who are susceptible to it reach their forties of fifties. This disease is characterized by a narrowing of the arteries, caused by the formation of plaques containing cells and cholesterol. Several factors influence the appearance of plaques, including high levels of cholesterol (and cholesterol precursors, such as triglyceride) in the blood, high blood pressure, and cigarette smoke.

Apolipoprotein E, encoded by a gene on chromosome 19, removes excess cholesterol from the blood by delivering it to liver cells, which store it for later use. Mutant apolipoprotein loses the ability to bind to liver receptors, resulting in a buildup of cholesterol in the blood. Several mutated forms of apolipoprotein E are known to occur and these need to be studied in detail before this disease can be treated with gene therapy.

A second form of cardiovascular disease, affecting the coronary arteries, is currently being treated with gene therapy. Coronary arteries carry blood to the myocytes, or heart muscle cells, and if they become blocked or otherwise damaged the cells die from lack of oxygen. In serious cases, this can lead to a massive heart attack and death of the patient. In milder cases, damage to the heart is minimal, but coronary circulation is insufficient to allow the patient a normal lifestyle. Gene therapy is attempting to help this group of patients by introducing directly into the heart a gene that codes for a blood vessel growth factor that stimulates both the growth and repair of the coronary arteries to reestablish an adequate blood flow.

Muscular Dystrophy

Muscular dystrophy, also called Duchenne muscular dystrophy (DMD), is one of a group of disorders characterized by a pathological swelling of skeletal muscles. It is caused by a mutation in the DMD gene, located on the X chromosome. DMD is the most prevalent form of this disease, occurring early in life and affecting nearly 1 million boys worldwide.

The gene for DMD codes for a protein called dystrophin, which is thought to strengthen muscle cells by anchoring the cytoskeleton to the surface membrane. Without dystrophin, the cell membrane becomes permeable to fluid entry, causing the cell to swell until it ruptures from the high internal pressure.

Researchers have developed a mouse model for DMD in an attempt to better understand the role of dystrophin in muscle physiology. Gene therapy trials are attempting to replace the mutated dystrophin or to introduce the closely related utrophin in order to stabilize the cell's membranes.

Alzheimer's Disease

Alzheimer's disease (AD) is a devastating neurological disorder that leads to a progressive loss of memory, language, and the ability to recognize friends and family. The average time course of the disease, from early symptoms to complete loss of cognition, is 10 years. Alois Alzheimer first described AD in 1907, and AD has since become the fourth leading cause of death among the elderly. The incidence of this disease increases with age, and it is twice as common in women than it is in men.

AD is a polygenic disease that tends to run in families and involves mutations in four genes, located on chromosomes 1, 14, 19, and 21. The best characterized, being the subject of many studies, is AD3 on chromosome 14, and AD4 on chromosome 1. These genes code for related cell-surface signaling proteins called amyloids, which, when mutated, become neurotoxins. A major characteristic of this disease is the formation of lesions, or wounds, made of fragmented brain cells surrounded by amyloid proteins. These lesions and their associated proteins are closely related to structures found in patients suffering from Down's syndrome, all of whom are affected by this disease.

Many scientists believe that AD is a single disease with a common metabolic amyloid pathway. That is, the four genetic loci associated with this disease all lead, when mutated, to the production of similar neurotoxic amyloid proteins. Gene therapy trials for this disease are in the planning stage.

Parkinson's Disease

This neurological disorder was first described by James Parkinson in 1817 and since then has become a serious health problem, with more than 500,000 North Americans affected at any one time. Most people are over 50 years old when the disease appears, although it can occur in younger patients. It is a neurodegenerative disease that manifests as a tremor, muscular stiffness, and difficulty with balance and walking. A typical feature of this disease is the presence of cellular debris, which consists of degenerating neurons, in several regions of the brain.

Until recently, Parkinson's disease was not thought to be heritable, and research was focused on environmental risk factors such as viral infection or neurotoxins. However, a candidate gene for some cases of Parkinson's disease was mapped to chromosome 4, and mutations in this gene have now been linked to several Parkinson's disease families.

The product of this gene is a protein called alpha-synuclein, which may also be involved in the development of Alzheimer's disease.

Since alpha-synuclein is implicated in both Parkinson's and Alzheimer's diseases, they may share a similar pathogenic mechanism. However, the function of this protein is not known, and for this reason gene therapy trials are still in the planning stage.

Huntington's Disease

Huntington's disease (HD) is an inherited neurological disease that leads to dementia in more than 30,000 North Americans every year. In addition, it has been estimated that 150,000 people are at risk of inheriting HD from their parents.

The HD gene was mapped to chromosome 4 in 1983 and cloned in 1993. The mutation is an expansion of a nucleotide triplet repeat (CAG-CAG-) in the DNA that codes for the protein Huntington. People who have the expanded CAG repeats always suffer from Huntington's disease, but the function of the gene product is not known. With the discovery of the HD gene, a test was developed that allows those at risk to find out whether or not they will develop the disease. Animal models have also been developed, and investigators know that mice have a gene that is similar to the human HD gene. Gene therapy trials for HD are in the planning stage. (See the gene therapy updates in chapter 8 for additional information.)

.2.

VIRUSES

The Cornerstone of Gene Therapy

Somebody once said that a virus is a piece of nucleic acid surrounded by bad news, and when we think of all the trouble these things have caused us over the years, we can easily see the truth in it. Viruses have given us such dread diseases as smallpox, polio, some forms of cancer, deadly influenza epidemics, the common cold, and AIDS. Yet, these masters of death and destruction are about to pay us back, in full and with interest. For without the viruses, there would be no gene therapy, and if we consider their ancestors, the plasmids, evolution of animal life on this planet would have been a much slower process.

When we speak of curing someone of a genetic disease, we are referring to gene replacement, or the process of introducing a normal gene into a defective cell. But how is this to be done? Eukaryotes are a clever bunch, and they take a dim view of foreign genes dropping by for lunch. To protect their privacy, they have surrounded themselves with a membrane that blocks the passive entry of everything except the tiniest of molecules. Even if a piece of DNA could gain access to the cell, it would still have to get into the nucleus before it could be replicated and transcribed. But the nucleus, like the cell, is surrounded by a lipid bilayer that also prevents passive diffusion of anything larger than a water molecule.

These are only a few of the problems that viruses had to overcome as they evolved into cellular parasites. Their first task was to find a way to get their genome into a cell, so the cell's machinery could be used to reproduce their kind. How they managed this, and how their success has become essential for the success of gene therapy, is the subject of this chapter.

Viruses Are Living Crystals

Soon after James Watson and Francis Crick resolved the structure of DNA, Watson published a paper on viral structure in which he sug-

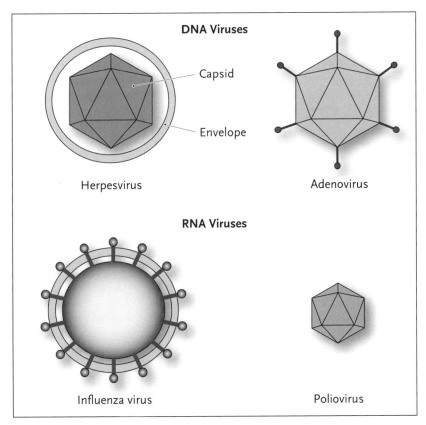

Viral morphology. Herpesvirus, adenovirus, and polioviruses all have icosahedral capsids, or protein coats, that surround and protect the viral genome, which may be DNA or RNA. Herpes and influenza viruses are also surrounded by a lipid bilayer that may be studded with proteins.

gested that since a virus is a tiny particle, less than one-tenth the size of a bacterium, it could only carry enough nucleic acid for a dozen or so genes. Consequently, he proposed that viral structure must consist of only a few proteins, used over and over again in some sort of symmetrical, highly ordered arrangement. To test this idea, many biologists examined viral structure under the newly available electron microscope, and when they did, they saw tiny crystalline structures that confirmed Watson's speculations.

We now know that most viruses, including the herpesvirus, adenovirus, and poliovirus, have a crystalline protein structure that is icosahedral (constructed from triangles, like a geodesic dome). The protein crystal forms a hollow compartment called the capsid that contains the viral genome. In some cases an envelope consisting of a lipid bilayer, which is often studded with proteins, surrounds the crystalline capsid. Some viruses, such as the influenza virus, have a simple, though highly ordered, spherical capsid instead of a crystalline icosahedron.

The presence or absence of an envelope, the structure of the capsid, and the nature of the viral genome—that is, whether it is RNA or DNA—are the most important characteristics scientists use to identify and classify these organisms.

Viral Genomes May Be RNA or DNA

All cells, whether they are prokaryotes or eukaryotes, have DNA genomes. DNA is a very stable molecule that can store many thousands of genes, essential for the complex lifestyles of modern cells, which often have 20,000 to 30,000 genes. In addition, double-stranded DNA allows for error correction, an extremely important feature when millions of nucleotides are to be replicated.

Viruses, on the other hand, are extremely simple organisms, so simple that many of them get by with fewer than a dozen genes. When genomes are this small, the advantage of DNA over RNA disappears. Consequently, viruses come with many different kinds of genomes, some using DNA, others RNA. They may be single-stranded or double, circular or linear. Viruses with only a few genes have a single-stranded RNA genome, but as the number of genes increases, the genome tends to be double-stranded DNA.

The adenovirus is a typical example of a DNA virus. This nonenveloped virus has a double-stranded DNA chromosome containing 30 to 40 genes that is capped at each end with a terminal protein offering

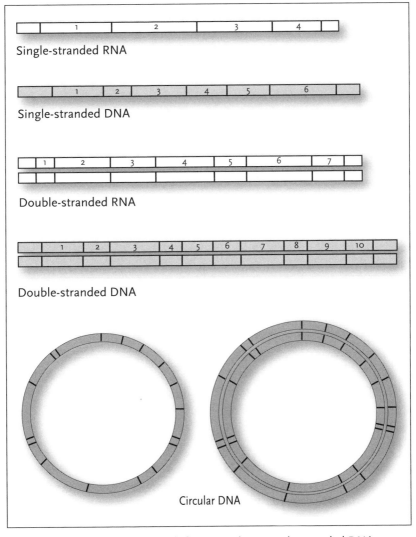

Single-stranded RNA

Single-stranded DNA

Double-stranded RNA

Double-stranded DNA

Circular DNA

Viral genomes. Small viruses with few genes have single-stranded DNA or RNA genomes. Large viruses with many genes always have double-stranded DNA genomes that are either linear or circular. In double-stranded genomes, one strand usually codes for all of the genes while the second strand provides stability and error correction.

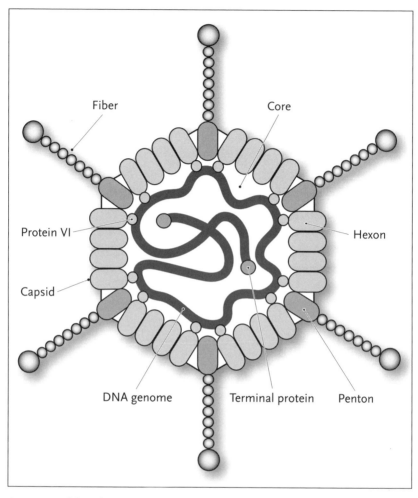

Structure of the adenovirus. The capsid is constructed from repeating hexon and penton proteins. A long fibrous protein, attached to each penton, is crucial for cell entry. The DNA chromosome, anchored by protein VI, contains 30 to 40 genes and is stabilized by two terminal proteins. Several other proteins, not shown, are stored in the core to initiate and maintain infection.

added stability to the molecule. The capsid is constructed from repeating hexon and penton (six- or five-sided) proteins. A protein filament with a bulbous tip is attached to each penton and plays an important role in getting the virus inside a cell. Most of the remaining genes code for proteins that are needed for infection. A few of the genes code for histonelike proteins that bind to the chromosome for added stability (histones and other cellular molecules are described in chapter 8). Adenoviruses, so named because they were originally isolated from the adenoid glands, cause the common cold and general infections of the upper respiratory tract.

The AIDS virus (HIV) is an example of an enveloped retrovirus that has an RNA genome. A retrovirus has a special enzyme called reverse transcriptase that converts the RNA chromosome to DNA after it infects a cell. This enzyme allows the virus to reverse the usual DNA-to-RNA

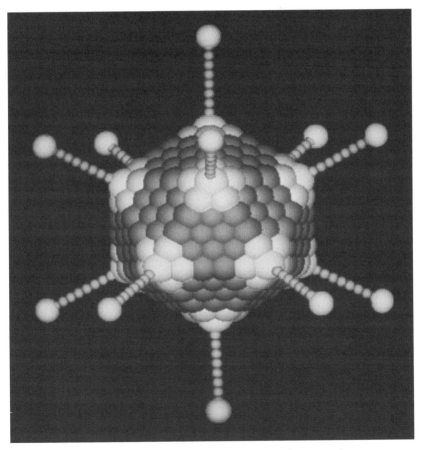

A computerized model of an adenovirus, a vector used in gene therapy. *(Science Source/Photo Researchers, Inc.)*

direction of genetic biosynthesis and is the reason they are called retro-viruses. The HIV capsid consists of a spherical protein matrix immediately beneath the envelope and a cone-shaped core that forms the genome compartment. The HIV genome consists of nine overlapping genes, three of which (*gag, pol,* and *env*) are common to all retroviruses.

Overlapping genes are unique to viruses. In such a genome, one stretch of the chromosome can be used to code for two or three genes. Viruses also process their mRNA to produce more than one protein from any given gene. When this occurs, a precursor mRNA is synthesized from the gene, after which it is split in half to produce two different proteins. Consequently, the *env* gene codes for two envelope proteins, glycoprotein (gp) 120 and 41 (the numbers refer to their

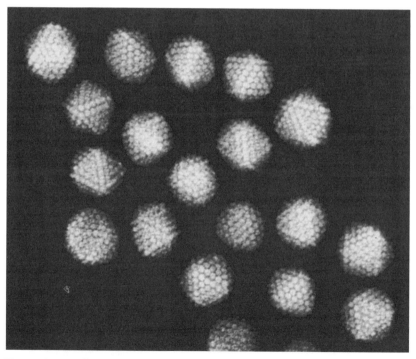

Transmission electron micrograph (TEM) of adenoviruses. These viruses normally attack the epithelial cells of the upper respiratory tract but are also known to cause pneumonia and conjunctivitis of the eye. Magnification: 200,000x. *(Meckes/Ottawa/Photo Researchers, Inc.)*

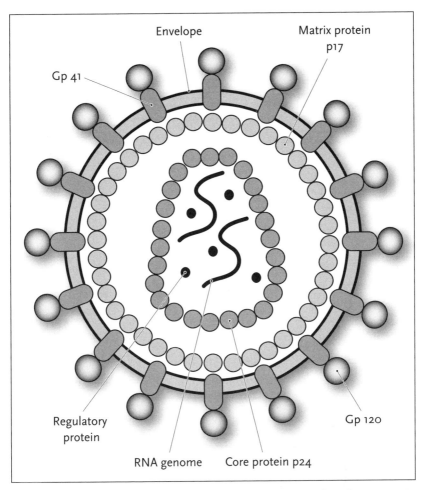

Structure of a retrovirus. The example shown is HIV, an enveloped retrovirus that has a double-stranded RNA genome containing nine genes. The capsid consists of a spherical matrix and an inner, cone-shaped protein core. Glycoproteins (Gp) 41 and 120, embedded in the envelope, are crucial for cell entry. Several regulatory proteins, including reverse transcriptase, are stored in the core.

relative sizes), and the *gag* gene codes for the matrix (p17) and core (p24) proteins. In addition, genes for six regulatory proteins overlap the *env* gene region of the chromosome. The *pol* gene codes for reverse transcriptase. Despite their simple structure and small genome,

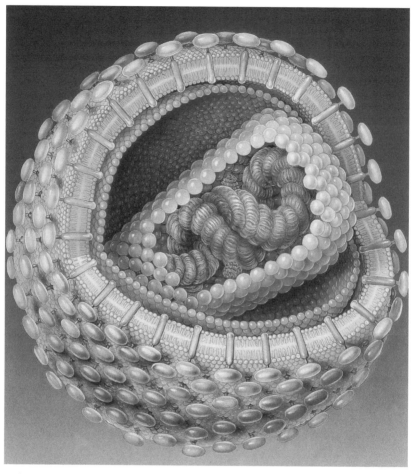

A three-dimensional cut-away drawing of the AIDS virus. Retroviruses such as this are commonly used as vectors in gene therapy. *(BSIP/Photo Researchers, Inc.)*

retroviruses are the most virulent pathogens known. Aside from AIDS, they are responsible for polio, smallpox, and several forms of cancer.

Viruses Evolved from Plasmids

It was once thought that because viruses are so simple, they must be extremely ancient and may have been the life-form that gave rise to the prokaryotes. But we know now that all viruses are cellular parasites, incapable of replicating their genome or of synthesizing their proteins without using cellular machinery. Consequently, they must have evolved after cells appeared, and their most likely ancestors are bacterial plasmids.

Plasmids are minichromosomes that bacteria have been swapping amongst themselves for more than 1 billion years. This form of prehistoric neighborly behavior was often of mutual benefit. Plasmids carry antibiotic resistance genes, so if a cell happens to make one that is particularly good, another, unrelated bacterium could get a copy simply by capturing the plasmid. Plasmids were probably released into the environment when a cell's membrane became leaky, for various reasons, or when the cell died and broke open, an event that echoes the molecular sharing that may have occurred among the prebiotic bubbles that gave rise to the first living cells. But plasmid exchange among prokaryotes could work only so long as the plasmids stayed small enough to reenter an intact cell by passive diffusion.

The first virus was probably a plasmid that picked up a gene for a protein that could spontaneously form a capsid. Acquiring a capsid made it possible for the virus to interact with cell-surface receptors, some of which are like doorways into the cell, so the virus was no longer dependent on passive diffusion for entry. In this sense, acquiring a capsid was like finding the key to the cell's door. Once the cell-surface barrier was removed, the viral genome was free to increase in size from a few genes to a few dozen. With a larger genome, viruses evolved a wide range of strategies for entering cells and, once inside, taking over cellular machinery to suit their own purposes.

Viruses Know How to Infect Cells

All cells need to communicate with the outside world, and in particular, they need a system for detecting and collecting food molecules. Prokaryotes satisfied these requirements by embedding protein receptors in their cell membrane. These receptors are part of a grander structure called the glycocalyx, a molecular forest that covers the cell membrane, reminiscent of the forests that once covered the surface of the Earth. With the establishment of the glycocalyx, the cell membrane became increasingly resistant to the passive diffusion of large molecules. That is, it tended not to leak as much as it did in primitive cells. This trend, begun by the prokaryotes, was converted to a rule by the eukaryotes: Anything coming in has to pass a port of entry.

Ports of entry include sugar receptors, hormone receptors, and ion channels. Ion channels are usually open, permitting free access to the

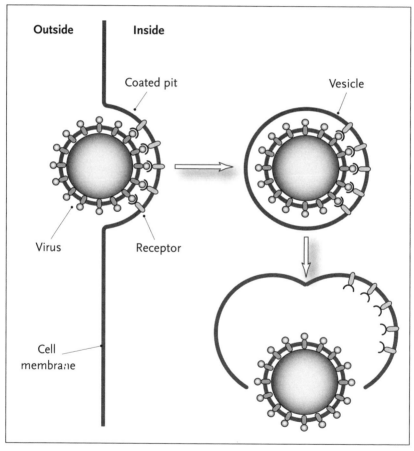

Receptor-mediated endocytosis. A virus enters a cell by binding to receptors in a coated pit, which activates endocytosis, a process the cell normally uses to ingest food or signaling molecules. Once inside, a viral enzyme attacks the wall of the vesicle, causing it to rupture, thus releasing the virus into the cytoplasm.

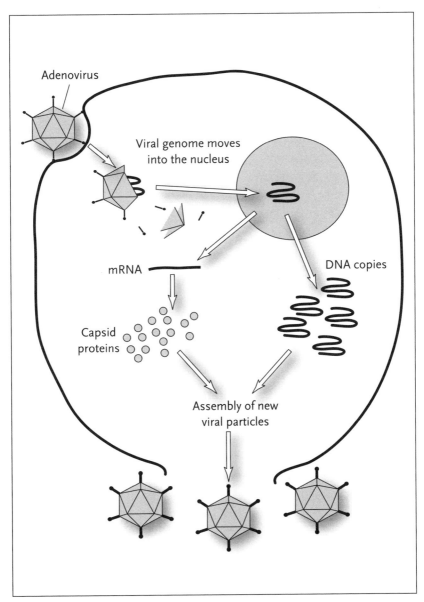

Life cycle of an adenovirus. After the virus enters the cell, the fragmented capsid docks at a nuclear pore (not shown) and releases the chromosome into the nucleus, where it is replicated and transcribed. The replicated DNA and the mRNA leave the nucleus and enter the cytoplasm. The viral mRNA is translated in the cytoplasm and the proteins join with the DNA copies to form new viral particles, which leave the cell by disrupting the membrane.

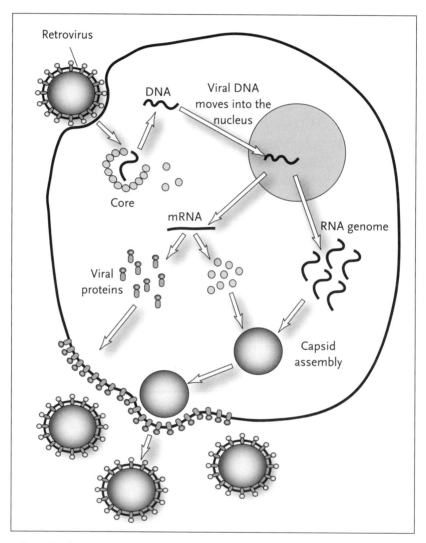

Life cycle of a retrovirus. After the virus enters the cell, the RNA chromosome is released from the core and copied into DNA by reverse transcriptase. The DNA chromosome enters the nucleus, where it integrates into a host chromosome, after which it is transcribed in RNA. The RNA leaves the nucleus, some of which is translated into capsid and envelope proteins, and the rest becomes new copies of the RNA genome. The translated viral proteins are embedded in the membrane. The assembled capsid obtains an envelope made of cell membrane and retroviral proteins while leaving the cell by exocytosis.

cell's interior, but the pore size is small enough to block entry to large molecules and microbes. The sugar receptors and some hormone receptors are linked to a process called endocytosis that is able to bring large molecules and microbes into the cell. When the proper molecule makes contact with these receptors, they are drawn inside by the formation of a vesicle (bubble). This type of entry is called receptor-mediated endocytosis.

Viral capsids can activate endocytosis to gain entry into a cell. Once inside, the virus releases an enzyme that attacks the wall of the vesicle, causing it to rupture, thus releasing the viral capsid into the cytoplasm. There are several variations to this scheme: For example, the AIDS virus binds to cell receptors but does not activate endocytosis. Instead, the viral envelope fuses with the cell membrane, releasing the capsid directly into the cytoplasm without the formation of a vesicle. In all cases, once the capsid is free in the cytoplasm, it breaks open to release the viral chromosome.

When an adenovirus enters a cell, the partially fragmented capsid binds to a nuclear pore, after which the chromosome moves into the nucleus, where it is replicated and transcribed. Viral mRNA and copies of its genome then move from the nucleus to the cytoplasm, where the mRNA is translated into capsid and other viral proteins. The replicated genome and the newly synthesized viral proteins auto-assemble into mature viral particles, which leave the cell by rupturing the cell membrane, killing the cell in the process.

The life cycle of a retrovirus is more complex than that of an adenovirus. When a retrovirus infects a cell, the capsid core breaks open to release the RNA genome into the cytoplasm, which is quickly converted to DNA by reverse transcriptase. The viral DNA moves into the nucleus and inserts itself into one of the cell's chromosomes. After insertion, the viral genes are transcribed, producing mRNA, and the entire length of viral DNA is transcribed to produce many copies of the viral RNA chromosome. The mRNA and the RNA chromosomes migrate back to the cytoplasm where the mRNA is translated into capsid, regulatory, and envelope proteins, the last-named of which is sent to the cell membrane by way of the endoplasmic reticulum and Golgi complex.

A transmission electron micrograph (TEM) of the AIDS virus (HIV) budding from an infected human T lymphocyte. Four viruses are seen in different stages of budding: At center left the virus acquires its coat from the cell membrane; at right the virus buds from the cell; at center right budding is almost complete; at left the new virus is free-floating. *(SPL/Photo Researchers, Inc.)*

New capsids form by the auto-assembly of the newly made RNA chromosomes and capsid proteins. The cell membrane, now studded with viral proteins, then forms an envelope around the viral particles as they leave the cell in a process called exocytosis. Thus, the lipid bilayer that surrounds this type of virus is obtained from the cell, while the envelope proteins are of viral origin. An important feature of this life cycle is that the virus does not rupture the membrane and hence does not kill the cell when it leaves.

The Virus as a Gene Vehicle

Given their talents for entering cells, viruses would appear to be ideal candidates for gene delivery vehicles or vectors. But there are two major problems to overcome before they can be used safely: First, the ability of the virus to replicate its own genome must be blocked, along with the production of viral mRNA that codes for proteins that maintain the infection and help the virus escape from the cell. Second, the therapeutic gene has to be inserted into the viral genome in such a way that it will not inhibit the formation of a normal capsid, since this is the part of the virus that is essential for cell entry.

Production of viral gene vehicles is carried out in a test tube. Viral genes needed for replication and the maintenance of infection are removed, after which the therapeutic gene is inserted into the viral chromosome. The hybrid chromosome is added to a test tube and mixed with purified viral capsid proteins, leading to the auto-assembly of viral particles. If this is done properly, the virus will be able to enter the cell to deliver the gene, but it will not harm the cell, nor will it be able to reproduce itself.

Viruses Used in Gene Therapy

Adenovirus type 2 (AD-2) and a retrovirus called murine (mouse) leukemia virus (MuLV) have been used in more than 90 percent of all gene therapy trials to date. AD-2, although naturally adapted to infecting the upper respiratory tract, has been used in trials that targeted T lymphocytes, liver, skin, and a variety of tumor cells. An important consideration when using this virus is the amount to give the patient. In a trial attempting to treat a liver ailment, for example, the recombinant AD-2 is injected directly into that organ. If the number of viral particles injected is correct, the liver receptors will bind up all of the viral particles. If the amount is too low, too few cells will take up the virus, so expression of the therapeutic gene will be insufficient to treat or cure the disease. If the amount is too high, viral particles will spill out into the general circulation and infect a variety of cells. Being crippled, these viruses cannot damage the cells they infect, but their presence can lead to a potentially deadly immune response as T cells detect and destroy infected cells. In extreme cases, this can lead to the destruction of entire organs and death of the patient.

While the adenovirus has proved to be a good delivery vehicle, the expression of the therapeutic gene tends to decline after a week or two.

This is believed to be due to the extrachromosomal life cycle of this virus. That is, the viral chromosome enters the cell nucleus, but it does not integrate into a host chromosome. Under these conditions, the cell's machinery does not continue transcribing the therapeutic gene. Moreover, AD vectors are inefficient at infecting some cells, and they tend to activate an antivector immune response.

Consequently, many clinical trials have turned to the retrovirus as an alternative vehicle. These viruses are very efficient at infecting cells of the immune system (the AIDS virus has made that perfectly clear) and they do not elicit as strong an immune response as do other vectors. Moreover, the retroviral life cycle includes integration of its genome into the host chromosome. Once it is in the chromosome, the therapeutic gene is expressed at a steady rate.

Unfortunately, in many cases, the rate at which a therapeutic gene is expressed by a retroviral vector is too low to cure the patient or even to

Illustration of an Ebola virus based on a scanning electron micrograph with a magnification of 130,000x. A number of major outbreaks of Ebola infections have occurred in equatorial Africa causing severe and frequently fatal hemorrhagic fever. Some scientists have proposed using this virus to produce novel vectors for gene therapy. *(Chris Bjornberg/Photo Researchers, Inc.)*

alleviate some of the symptoms. In addition, there is always some apprehension about using an integrating virus, because if something goes wrong, there is, at present, no way to get it out again. This is particularly worrisome, since in an attempt to increase expression of the therapeutic gene, some gene therapy trials use retroviral vectors that are replication competent (can still reproduce).

The justification for designing replication-competent retroviral vectors is that these viruses do not kill the cell when they exit. If its pathology-inducing genes are removed, reproduction of the vector and its movement from cell to cell are of no concern. Vector reproduction leads to an increased number of cells being infected and thus increases the amount of therapeutic protein being synthesized, with subsequent benefits for the patient. However, there is always the possibility that one of these vectors will encounter another virus infecting the patient and, through genetic recombination, become pathogenic and possibly deadly.

An alternative approach involves genetic engineering of hybrid retroviruses that might produce large quantities of the therapeutic protein while being unable to replicate themselves. To this end, scientists have recently created an Ebola-HIV viral hybrid to be used as a novel gene delivery vehicle. Scientists know that both viruses are deadly and exceptionally talented when it comes to infecting cells. The hybrid appears to work well in animal experimentation, but whether it will ever be approved for use in human gene therapy trials is another question. Crippled though the vector is, the scare factor associated with it is such that many people will be reluctant to have it injected into their veins.

·3·

ASHI DeSILVA

A Promising Start

Dr. Michael Blaese and Dr. French Anderson of the National Institutes of Health (NIH) conducted the first gene therapy trial. In 1990 there were only two patients in that trial: The first was Ashanthi DeSilva, who was then just four years old; the second was a nine-year-old girl who, because of a wish to remain anonymous, is referred to simply as patient 2. Patient 2 showed only modest improvements following the treatment, but for DeSilva, it was a dramatic success.

Both patients suffered from a genetic disease called severe combined immunodeficiency (SCID), briefly described in chapter 2. SCID is an immune system disorder that makes it very difficult for those afflicted to fight off even mild diseases, such as the common cold or influenza. The term *combined immunodeficiency* refers to the involvement of both the T and B lymphocytes. The term *severe* was used in the original descriptions of this disease because most children had a severe clinical disease and died before their second birthday. However, by the time DeSilva was treated, diagnosis and improved treatments (other than gene therapy) meant that most children lived much longer. Today, the term *severe* refers more to the lifestyle that SCID patients have to endure, rather than an early death.

The particular form of SCID that DeSilva and patient 2 suffered from was due to a deficiency in an enzyme called adenosine deaminase (ADA). The gene for this enzyme is located on the long arm of chromosome 20. Humans, being diploid creatures, receive a copy of each chromosome from both parents; this is nature's way of protecting us from genetic abnormalities. A child who receives a defective ADA gene from one parent and a healthy ADA gene from the other parent will not develop SCID, because the defective gene is recessive to the normal gene. That is, the normal gene makes a functional copy of the protein, thus compensating for the defective copy made by the mutated gene. This is why ADA deficiency is referred to as an autosomal recessive genetic defect and why genetic diseases, in general, are rare. Symptoms occur only if the child receives a defective ADA gene from both parents.

The standard treatment for ADA deficiency is a bone marrow transplant or a drug called PEG-ADA that supplies normal copies of the enzyme to the patient. Bone marrow transplants were not possible for DeSilva or patient 2 owing to the lack of compatible donors. Both patients were being treated with PEG-ADA in the months leading up to the trial. Indeed, this treatment was a requirement for entry into the trial, as it improved their health, which would be beneficial in the event of any side effects resulting from the trial. Although PEG-ADA relieves many of the symptoms of SCID, it is not a cure. The drug provides an extracellular source of normal ADA, but the internal environment of each B and T lymphocyte is still deficient. Consequently, even with ADA supplements the immune system does not function normally.

Both patients were admitted to the trial in the hope that gene therapy would cure their disease. DeSilva responded remarkably well to the treatment, but as we will see, the trial itself was but the tip of a scientific iceberg, based on preliminary research stretching back to the early 1970s. This work included the identification of ADA as the source of the clinical symptoms, isolation of the ADA gene, and years of work that clarified the role of this gene and how the genetic defect led to a crippled immune system. Preliminary research was also concerned with the details of the gene therapy procedure: the type of virus used as the gene vehicle, the joining of the isolated ADA gene to the virus, and the method used to deliver the ADA-virus construct to the patient. These things all had to be worked out in detail, using animal models, before gene therapy could be used to treat a human patient.

Clinical Trials Defined

Clinical trials are conducted in four phases and are always preceded by research conducted on experimental animals such as mice, rats, or monkeys. The format for preclinical research is informal; it is conducted in a variety of research labs around the world, with the results being published in scientific journals. Formal approval from a governmental regulatory body is not required.

PHASE I CLINICAL TRIAL

Pending the outcome of the preclinical research, investigators may apply for permission to try the experiments on human subjects. Applications in the United States are made to the Food and Drug Administration (FDA), the National Institutes of Health (NIH), and the Recombinant DNA Advisory Committee (RAC). RAC was set up by NIH to monitor any research, including clinical trials, dealing with cloning, recombinant DNA, or gene therapy. Phase I trials are conducted on a small number of adult volunteers, usually between two and 20, who have given informed consent. That is, the investigators explain the procedure, the possible outcomes, and especially the dangers associated with the procedure before the subjects sign a consent form. The purpose of the Phase I trial is to determine the overall effect the treatment has on humans. A treatment that works well in monkeys or mice may not work at all on humans. Similarly, a treatment that appears safe in lab animals may be toxic, even deadly, when given to humans. Since most clinical trials are testing a new drug of some kind, the first priority is to determine a safe dosage for humans. Consequently, subjects in the Phase I trial are given a range of doses, all of which, even the high dose, are less than the highest dose given to experimental animals. If the results from the Phase I trial are promising, the investigators may apply for permission to proceed to Phase II.

PHASE II CLINICAL TRIAL

Having established the general protocol, or procedure, the investigators now try to replicate the encouraging results from Phase I, but with a much larger number of subjects (100–300). Only with a large number of subjects is it possible to prove the treatment has an effect. In addition, dangerous side effects may have been missed in Phase I because of a small sample size. The results from Phase II will determine how safe the procedure is and whether it works. If the statistics show that the treatment is effective and toxicity is low, the investigators may apply for permission to proceed to Phase III.

PHASE III CLINICAL TRIAL

Based on Phase II results the procedure may look very promising, but before it can be used as a routine treatment it must be tested on thousands of patients at a variety of research centers. This is the expensive part of bringing a new drug or therapy to market; it can cost millions, sometimes billions, of dollars. It is for this reason that Phase III clinical trials invariably have the financial backing of large pharmaceutical or biotechnology companies. If the results of the Phase II trial are confirmed in Phase III, the FDA will approve the use of the drug for routine treatment. The use of the drug or treatment now passes into an informal Phase IV trial.

PHASE IV CLINICAL TRIAL

Even though the treatment has gained formal approval, its performance is monitored for very long-term effects, sometimes stretching on for 10–20 years. In this way, the FDA retains the power to recall the drug long after it has become a part of standard medical procedure. It can happen that in the long term, the drug costs more than an alternative, in which case health insurance providers may refuse to cover the cost of the treatment.

Cells of the Immune System

The human immune system is composed of a diverse group of white blood cells that are divided into three major categories: granulocytes, monocytes, and lymphocytes. Granulocytes have a distinctive lobular nucleus, and all are phagocytic. Monocytes are large phagocytic cells, with an irregularly shaped nucleus. The largest monocytes, the macrophages, can engulf whole bacteria as well as damaged, or senescent, body cells. Lymphocytes have a smooth morphology and a large, round nucleus. T lymphocytes and natural killer (NK) cells deal primarily

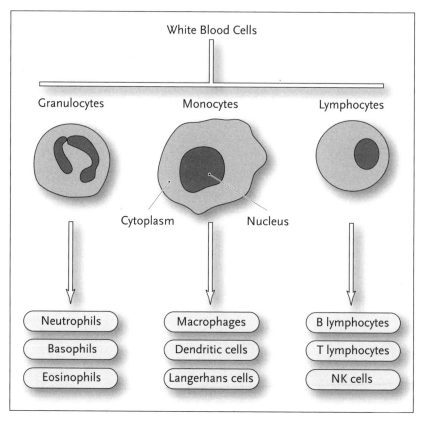

White blood cells. These cells are divided into three major categories: granulocytes, monocytes, and lymphocytes. Granulocytes have a distinctive, lobular nucleus and are phagocytic (they eat cells, viruses, and debris). Monocytes are large cells with an irregularly shaped nucleus. All monocytes are phagocytic; the largest members, the macrophages, can engulf whole bacteria and damaged or senescent body cells. Lymphocytes have a smooth morphology with a large round nucleus. B lymphocytes are nonphagocytic but produce antibodies. T lymphocytes and natural killer (NK) cells coordinate the immune response and can force infected cells to commit suicide.

with coordinating the immune response and killing already infected body cells. B lymphocytes are nonphagocytic; they deal with an invading microbe by releasing antibodies.

Phagocytosis of an invading microbe by granulocytes and monocytes represents a first-line defense called the innate response. All animals

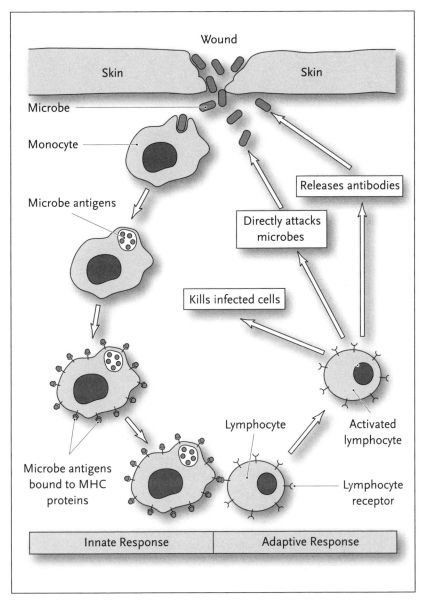

Innate and adaptive immune response. Phagocytosis of invading microbes is called the innate response. In higher vertebrates, microbe antigens, bound to special monocyte surface proteins called the major histocompatibility complex (MHC), are then presented to lymphocytes. Contact between the lymphocyte receptor and the antigen activates the lymphocyte and the adaptive response, consisting of a three-pronged attack on the microbe and microbe-infected cells.

are capable of mounting this kind of defense. Activation of the lymphocytes leads to a more powerful second line of defense, the adaptive response, which is found only in higher vertebrates and is initiated by monocytes, specifically dendritic and Langerhans cells. These cells, after engulfing a virus or bacterium, literally tear the microbe apart and then embed the pieces, now called antigens, in their membrane. The antigens are presented to lymphocytes, which become activated when their receptors bind to the microbial antigens. Activated B lymphocytes secrete antibodies specifically designed to combat that particular microbe. Activated T cells and NK cells attack the microbe directly, but are primarily concerned with locating and killing infected body cells.

The adaptive system can remember a pathogen long after it has been removed from the body. This is why a specific bacteria or virus strain cannot make us sick twice. Once infected, we develop a natural lifelong immunity. We can also immunize ourselves against many diseases by injecting a crippled version of the pathogen, or specific antigens from a pathogen, into our bloodstream. This concoction of bits and pieces from a pathogen, called an immunizing serum, will activate the adaptive response, giving us a lasting, though not always lifelong, immunity against the disease. The adaptive system, consisting of activated B and T lymphocytes, is extremely powerful, and it is this system that is destroyed by adenosine deaminase deficiency, for the lack of this enzyme cripples both the B and T lymphocytes.

The activities of a healthy immune system, particularly the function of T lymphocytes and NK cells, have a direct bearing on the outcome of a gene therapy trial. The immune system will attack and destroy anything that is foreign, and that includes a viral vector carrying a therapeutic gene. We will see just how much this can complicate an otherwise straightforward procedure.

Adenosine Deaminase (ADA)

Adenosine deaminase (ADA) is an enzyme involved in the purine salvage pathway. Purines, such as adenine and guanine, are structural components of nucleotides. The cell recycles these molecules continuously, using them to construct new nucleotides, fats, or proteins. Decomposition of a nucleotide begins with the removal of the phosphates by a nucleotidase and the removal of an amino group on the purine by ADA. The molecule that is left behind, called inosine, is broken down further by other enzymes. Inosine components, the free phosphates, and the

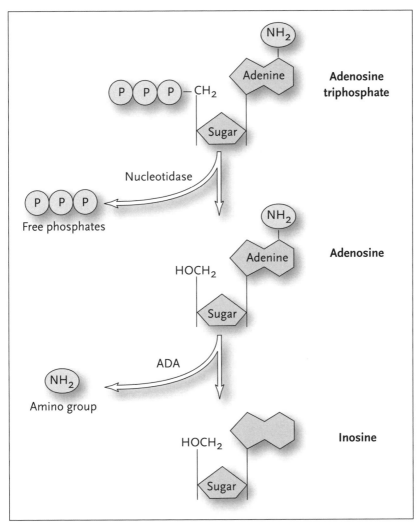

Recycling adenosine triphosphate. Disassembly begins with the removal of the phosphates by a nucleotidase to produce the nucleoside adenosine, followed by the removal of the amino group by adenosine deaminase (ADA) to produce inosine. All three components are recycled to make new nucleotides and amino acids.

amino group are all recycled. In the absence of ADA, adenosine concentrations build up to toxic levels, damaging both the B and T lymphocytes and impeding their replication, and thus making it impossible for them to mount an effective immune response.

Preliminary Research

Studies involving ADA and its role in SCID can be traced back to the 1970s. These very early studies were concerned with the identification of the defective enzyme and which cells of the immune system were affected. Between 1972 and 1978 ADA was identified as the enzyme responsible for the disease, and a buildup of adenosine was shown to be specifically toxic to T and B lymphocytes.

The ADA gene was isolated and sequenced in 1985, and several mutations were identified by 1989. During this same time period, methods were being developed to treat ADA deficiency with bone marrow transplants and infusions of PEG-ADA, the drug that temporarily supplies copies of ADA. Both of these procedures help some patients, but each comes with its own set of problems and disadvantages. The major problem associated with transplants is finding a suitable donor. Even if such a donor is found, there is still the possibility the transplant will be rejected or will cause serious side effects.

PEG-ADA is a drug that is produced by linking ADA to a molecule called polyethylene glycol (PEG), which increases its stability in the patient's bloodstream. Pure ADA has a half-life of only 30 minutes to one hour, while PEG-ADA can last for up to two to three days. The drug has to be injected directly into the bloodstream, meaning that young children must be subjected to an unpleasant procedure every other day for all of their lives. Moreover, as already noted, the drug does not cure the disease, and children receiving the drug are still incapable of mounting an effective immune response to a variety of diseases.

To deal with the shortcomings of the standard treatment, Anderson and Blaese began to explore the possibility of treating ADA deficiency with gene therapy as early as 1987 when they submitted their first proposal, for a Phase I trial, to NIH and RAC, based on preclinical results from monkeys. The review process, then as now, was extremely rigorous. The proposal was reviewed by at least a dozen scientists, who made recommendations that had to be addressed before RAC would approve the trial. Among the recommendations were three primary concerns that RAC had regarding the safety of the procedure:

1. The number of transduced cells (cells infected with the vector-ADA gene) obtained in monkey gene transfer models was very low and there was no evidence that totipotent stem cells, the optimal target cells, had been transduced.

2. Even though the ADA gene was expressed efficiently in mature ADA-deficient T cells in tissue culture, there was no evidence that the gene would remain active during the differentiation of T cell precursors to the final mature T cell found in general circulation.

3. The ADA vector preparation available at that time was contaminated with a helper virus (a virus that helps insert the ADA gene into the vector), and there were only preliminary in vivo primate data (obtained from monkeys) suggesting that a helper virus might not pose a public health risk.

These questions, together with the success of PEG-ADA treatment and the fact that the protocol called for the treatment of infants, led the RAC to conclude that additional work was needed to confirm the safety of the virus and the protocol in adult subjects before it could be used to treat infants or children. Accordingly, Blaese and Anderson were given permission in 1989 to conduct a Phase I clinical trial using adult human cancer patients. The basic layout of the procedure included the following: lymphocytes, isolated from the patients, were transformed with retrovirus and then returned to the donor patient. Adults were used in this trial because the dangers could be fully explained to them, meeting the requirements regarding informed consent.

The trial was intended to confirm the safety of the vector and the infusion procedure in human subjects, both of which had been tested extensively in mice and rhesus monkeys that had received infusions of ADA transgenic lymphocytes. As an added precaution, the vector used in the human cancer trial did not carry a therapeutic gene, but it did carry the marker sequence NeoR, so the investigators could follow the fate of the vector and proliferation of the infused cells. They found that the NeoR gene remained active for up to five months.

The information collected in the cancer trial suggested that a therapeutic gene would remain active for long periods and could be expected to improve the clinical symptoms of a disease such as ADA deficiency. In addition, none of the six trial patients experienced abnormalities, side effects, toxicities, or pathology due to the retroviral-mediated gene transfer procedure, thus confirming the earlier results with mice and monkeys. Based on these results, the RAC gave formal approval for a Phase I trial to treat ADA deficiency in children.

Clinical Procedure for ADA Gene Therapy

The procedure begins with the removal of some T lymphocytes from patients being treated with PEG-ADA. The T cells are grown in tissue culture, and a normal ADA gene is inserted into them using a process called retroviral-mediated gene transfer, after which the gene-corrected cells are returned to the patient. The vector is a modified murine leukemia virus (retrovirus) called LASN, into which the ADA gene has been inserted.

The protocol was designed to have two parts. In part 1, low numbers of gene-corrected T lymphocytes were given to the patient repeatedly in order to build up the immune system and also to obtain information as to how long gene-corrected T cells survive. In part 2A, a selection procedure was used to increase the number of gene-corrected T cells making substantial amounts of the ADA enzyme. These enriched cells were then given to the patient monthly for approximately six months. In part 2B, the number of gene-corrected T cells were increased to the predicted therapeutic level (about 1 billion gene-corrected T cells per kilogram body weight of the patient). Then, 1 billion to 3 billion gene-corrected T cells per kilogram were infused several times, after which the patient was monitored in order to determine if the immune system was functioning normally.

The DeSilva Clinical Trial

In 1990 Ashi DeSilva became one of two patients enrolled in the first-ever gene therapy trial. Blaese and Anderson led the trial, which involved a total of 30 principal investigators and nursing personnel. DeSilva's lymphocytes were isolated, grown in culture, and transduced with the LASN vector containing the ADA gene, as already described. Almost from the first day of the trial, her immune response improved. Transfusions were continued for two years, after which her response to the trial was closely monitored. In 1995 Blaese and several colleagues published a detailed account of the trial in the journal *Science*. Both Patient 2 and DeSilva showed an improvement, but DeSilva's response exceeded everyone's expectations. Within five to six months of beginning the trial, DeSilva's T cell count rapidly increased and stabilized in the normal range. ADA enzyme activity, nearly undetectable in her lymphocytes initially, increased in concentration during the first two years of treatment, reaching a level roughly half that of a normal value, making it possible for her to lead a normal life.

DeSilva's immune response has diminished somewhat since the trial but as of 2003, when she was 17 years old, it remained within the normal range. The reduction in her immune response may be due to an autoimmune response that is leading to the destruction of some of her own T lymphocytes. This can happen if monocytes encounter vector antigens and present them to T lymphocytes, thus activating an adaptive response against the vector and any cells containing it. In this particular case, the autoimmune response would be mild, since the retrovirus generally remains in the nucleus, thus minimizing exposure of its antigens.

The DeSilva trial proved that gene therapy can be used to cure certain genetic diseases. Interest in the procedure increased dramatically from only a few trials in the early 1990s to more than 600 trials in 2004. Most of these trials are designed to treat various forms of cancer, but a few are attempting to cure SCID by combining gene therapy with stem cell therapy. Between 2000 and 2002, Italian, British, and French medical teams, using transgenic stem cells, reported complete success in curing patients suffering from SCID-ADA and SCID-X1, an interleukin-deficient form of SCID (described in chapter 1). These teams have all used improved versions of the LASN vector that Anderson and his colleagues developed; this, coupled with the use of transgenic stem cells, has greatly improved the percentage of successful outcomes. In this approach, isolated stem cells are transfected with the therapeutic gene and then injected into the patient, where they differentiate into mature T lymphocytes possessing improved functionality. In the British trial, for example, eight out of nine patients showed dramatic improvements in the function of their immune response. However, all of these trials are still at the Phase II or III level, and have yet to be approved as a standard therapy. (See gene therapy updates in chapter 8.)

·4·

JESSE GELSINGER
Down to Earth

Throughout the 1990s, the gene therapy community was riding a wave of euphoria brought on by the great success of the DeSilva trial. Even though there were some in the science community who complained that gene therapy offered more than it could deliver, most observers were impressed with the accomplishments and the potential benefit such a procedure could bring to medical practice.

Critics, however, pointed out that the performance of gene therapy between 1990 and 1998 was of little consequence. Several trials had been launched to cure other patients of SCID-ADA without success, reducing the initial success rate to one in 20. Even so, the potential for gene therapy continued to be held in high regard, and the number of trials increased from one in 1990 to more than 300 in 1998. Most scientists were not concerned with the low success rate. They realized that with such a novel and complex therapy, it could take several decades before the wrinkles were ironed out of the protocols. In addition, there was general agreement that the DeSilva trial had made the crucial point: Gene therapy works. It is only a matter of time before the procedure is refined enough that it will work for everyone.

It was during this euphoric period in 1995 that the University of Pennsylvania set up its Institute for Human Gene Therapy (IHGT) and hired Dr. Jim Wilson as its director. Wilson, in turn, hired Dr. Mark Batshaw, a physician long interested in gene therapy who had devised one of the first drugs to treat OTC deficiency, a genetic disease that affects the liver. Batshaw convinced Wilson to make OTC deficiency the subject of their first gene therapy trial, and they began by studying the properties of various viruses that might serve as a gene therapy vectors. Rather than use the LASN vector or another retrovirus, they decided to use an adenovirus (AD virus), because in animal models it seemed to be a more efficient vector. In 1997, after a year spent working out the details of their procedure, they applied for and were granted permission to conduct a Phase I gene therapy trial to correct OTC deficiency in adult patients.

The trial began in fall 1998 with 18 patients enrolled. The 18th patient—at age 18, the youngest volunteer—was Jesse Gelsinger. The trial was terminated a year later, just four days after Gelsinger was treated. On the second day of his treatment, Gelsinger lapsed into a coma, and 24 hours later he was pronounced dead. Within days of Gelsinger's death, NIH ordered a halt to all AD-vector gene therapy trials being conducted in the United States. The ban lasted a full year and was accompanied by an investigation that was not concluded until fall 2001. Gene therapy was placed on trial, certainly the most rigorous trial any medical procedure has ever had to endure. For a time it looked as though Gelsinger's death was also the death of a promising therapy, and the end of Wilson and Batshaw's careers.

Ornithine Transcarbamylase (OTC)

OTC is a liver enzyme that rids the body of toxic ammonia, which is generated when our cells recycle protein. The first step in the recycling process liberates free amino acids; the second step involves the release of an amino group (NH_2) that is found on every amino acid. The amino group is quickly converted to ammonia (NH_3 or NH_4) with the addition of one or two hydrogen atoms. The ammonia is ultimately converted to urea by the liver in a series of biochemical reactions known as the urea cycle. The kidneys readily excrete urea in the urine, from which urine gets its name.

Ammonia enters the urea cycle when it, along with carbon dioxide, is added to ornithine to produce citrulline; this crucial step in the cycle is catalyzed by OTC. When OTC is defective, ammonia levels build up in

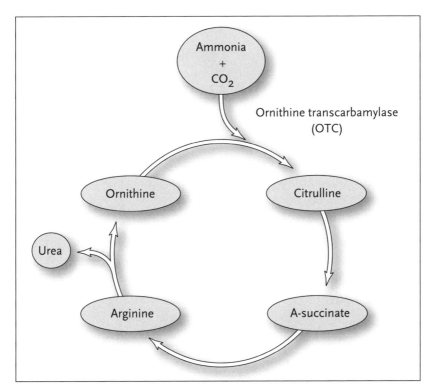

The urea cycle. Cells in the liver rid the body of toxic ammonia by converting it to urea, which is then excreted by the kidneys as urine. Ammonia and carbon dioxide (CO_2) are added to ornithine to produce citrulline, a reaction that is catalyzed by the enzyme OTC. Other enzymes in the cycle produce argininosuccinate (A-succinate) and arginine; the latter is split into urea and ornithine, thus completing the cycle.

the blood, resulting in convulsions, vomiting and coma, with death following quickly if treatment is not administered. The central nervous system is especially vulnerable to ammonia levels, because neurons, being extremely energetic, require a constant supply of ATP (the molecule that all cells use as the ultimate source of energy). Ammonia blocks the production of ATP, leading quickly to the death of neurons and other especially active cells, such as muscle cells and cells of the digestive tract. Convulsions and vomiting are early signs of energy-starved muscle and intestinal cells.

Preliminary Research

Ammonia intoxication, referred to as hyperammonemic syndrome (or hyperammonemia), was described in the early 1960s, and was quickly connected to a defect in the urea cycle. The urea cycle is a series of biochemical reactions that was discovered by Hans Krebs and Kurt Henseleit in 1932, five years before Krebs described the many reactions involved in the citric acid cycle.

The urea cycle was the first cyclic metabolic pathway to be discovered. It consists of five enzymes, defects in any one of which can cripple the liver's ability to produce urea. Mutations have been described for all of the urea cycle enzymes, but throughout the 1980s it became clear that OTC deficiency was by far the most common mutation, accounting for more than 40 percent of all mutations affecting urea production. It is also the most lethal. Patients suffering from mutations in other urea cycle enzymes, leading to a buildup of citrulline or arginine, for example, are easily treated, and rarely suffer the life-threatening coma that is associated with increased ammonia concentrations in the blood.

OTC deficiency, and the study of it, brings us around to the grand ecological association between animals, plants, and prokaryotes, all focused on the utilization of nitrogenous compounds and the problems organisms have when trying to recycle them. Ammonia and amino acids, both nitrogenous compounds, were produced in the stormy environment of prebiotic Earth. When the first cells appeared, they found themselves in an environment rich in these compounds. Amino acids could be used directly to form simple proteins, and as the original supply of amino acids was depleted, cells learned how to manufacture their own amino acids by using ammonia from the atmosphere. Eventually, the atmospheric ammonia was depleted (something we are all grateful for now), but by that time, prokaryotes and certain plants had evolved that could capture molecular nitrogen from the atmosphere, a process called nitrogen fixation. By capturing nitrogen from the atmosphere, these organisms ensured a ready supply of nitrogenous compounds for all living things in the ecosystem.

There is, of course, a limited amount of nitrogen in our ecosystem; plants return theirs to the ecosystem when they die and decompose. Animals likewise return nitrogen to the ecosystem when they die, but they also return a great deal of it, throughout their lives, as urine. Animals produce the urine by way of recycling amino acids, and when they do, it is as though they are resurrecting the Earth's ancient, ammonia-rich atmosphere. Because of its toxicity, early cells quickly learned to convert the free ammonia to urea, thus giving birth to the urea cycle.

Genetic defects affecting the urea cycle in general, and OTC in particular, are fairly common, affecting one in 40,000 male children every year in the United States alone. Consequently, the hunt for the OTC gene began almost as soon as recombinant DNA technology made the effort a possibility. By 1989 the gene for OTC had been isolated, several mutations described in detail, and its location on the X chromosome confirmed. The OTC gene, because of its location, is referred to as being X-linked, and as a consequence, the most serious cases are always among males, who have a single X chromosome, in contrast to females, who have two. Women are usually asymptomatic carriers, but do occasionally suffer a mild form of the disease owing to the random inactivation of one of their X chromosomes (for genetic stability, human females, like their male counterparts, have one functional X chromosome per cell). Mild forms of OTC deficiency can occur in males as the result of a random mutation that damages the OTC gene in some, but not all, liver cells, thus producing somatic cells (that is, liver cells) mosaic for the OTC gene (some cells in the liver are normal, while some are defective). This is the form of the disease that Jesse Gelsinger suffered from, and it is generally referred to as a partial deficiency of OTC.

Clinical Procedure for OTC Gene Therapy

There are substantial differences between OTC gene therapy and the clinical procedure described for ADA deficiency. OTC is not located in single blood-borne cells as in ADA. Instead, this particular genetic abnormality affects an organ; consequently, it is not practical to collect a few liver cells, transfect them with the corrected gene, and then return them to the body (although this is possible with certain kinds of stem cells). Instead, OTC gene therapy involves the injection of the viral vector into the blood or directly into the liver, which, it is hoped, will transfect liver cells, thus curing, or at least treating, the disease.

Another difference is that OTC gene therapy is administered using an adenovirus (AD virus) rather than a retrovirus, as is used to treat ADA deficiencies. The AD virus causes upper respiratory tract infections, the common cold, and conjunctivitis (eye infection), all of which are usually mild infections (for further discussion of the AD virus, see chapter 2). Gene therapists believe that the AD virus is a more potent vector in that it supports expression of the transgene (in this case, the OTC gene) at therapeutic levels. That is, the amount of OTC produced will either cure the disease or result in an obvious reduction of the clinical symptoms.

After OTC patients are injected with the virus, they must be carefully monitored for toxic side effects of the treatment and for any improvement in ammonia metabolism. Toxicity is evaluated by determining the biochemical behavior of the liver, blood concentrations of ammonia and urea, urine output, and general kidney function. The patients' white blood cell count, which serves as an indicator of immune response, is also determined. Potential risks that gene therapists prepare for include direct or immune-mediated injuries to the liver, kidneys, heart, and lungs.

Wilson's team at the University of Pennsylvania Hospital developed a protocol for their first gene therapy trial, in which an AD vector was to be administered to 18 patients by direct infusion into the right hepatic (liver) artery. Delivery rates and volume of instillation were to be kept constant for all participants. Cohorts of three subjects would be assigned to six dosing regimens, with each cohort receiving a progressively higher dose of vector, adjusted for the body weight of each subject. The first two participants in each cohort were to be females, with male subjects eligible only as the third subject in each cohort. Doses ranged from 1.4×10^{11} vector particles to 3.8×10^{13}. The vector was to be administered to the cohorts in tandem; that is, cohort 1 would be dosed and monitored before treatment began on cohort 2 (this is the reason the trial had been under way for a full year before Gelsinger was treated). Within each cohort the female subjects would receive the virus before the males. Dosing the patients in this way made it possible to incorporate several stopping rules. For example, if cohort 1 suffered toxic side effects, either cohort 2 would not be treated or it would be treated with a lower dose. If the female subjects within any cohort suffered severe side effects, the male subjects would not be treated. The rationale for this stopping rule is that the female carriers of OTC deficiency, being heterozygous, are generally in better health than symptomatic males and thus better able to deal with toxic side effects.

The Gelsinger Clinical Trial

On September 9, 1999, Jesse Gelsinger caught a flight from his home in Arizona to Philadelphia, Pennsylvania. His father, Paul Gelsinger, was to join him shortly after the trial began. On Monday morning, September 13, Gelsinger checked into the hospital at the University of Pennsylvania and was taken to the Interventional Radiology Suite, where he was sedated and a catheter was passed into his liver from a vein in his groin. At 10:30 A.M., the attending surgeon, Dr. Steve Raper, attached a syringe to the catheter and slowly injected 30 ml of an AD vector carrying the OTC gene.

Gelsinger was the second patient in cohort 6, receiving the highest dose of 3.8×10^{13} vector particles. Injecting the vector directly into the liver was thought to be safer than injecting it into general circulation. If the treatment went as planned, liver receptors would bind all of the viral particles, thus minimizing the exposure of the rest of the body to the vector. Infusion of the vector was complete by 12:30 P.M. That night, Gelsinger developed a fever and became sick to his stomach, an expected early reaction. By early Tuesday morning, however, his condition became serious. He was disoriented, and the whites of his eyes had turned yellow, an early sign of liver damage and possible onset of a clotting disorder called disseminated intravascular coagulation (DIC).

The normal, daily turnover of red blood cells (RBCs) is the link between yellowing eyes and liver damage. When RBCs are recycled, a major breakdown product is a yellowish compound called bilirubin, which is normally broken down by the liver. If the liver is damaged, the concentration of bilirubin in the blood increases very quickly, thus affecting the color of the eyes. The destruction of RBCs can be unnaturally high in a patient suffering from DIC, which accelerates the rate at which bilirubin accumulates. DIC is a complex syndrome that is usually triggered by a massive bacterial or viral infection, and is initiated by monocytes as part of the innate immune response. Serious trouble begins with the activation of the adaptive system. Because the infection is so severe, T lymphocytes and NK cells begin killing large numbers of infected cells—so many, in fact, that it inflicts serious damage to entire organs. Complicating matters, the T lymphocytes release an enormous number of communication molecules, called interleukins, to maximize the extent of the adaptive response. The high concentration of interleukins, however, stimulates inappropriate coagulation of the blood throughout the circulatory system. The system-wide formation of blood clots blocks the flow of blood through the capillaries, thus depriving tissues of nutrients and oxygen. The end result, in Gelsinger's case, was tissue swelling and multiorgan failure.

The problem of DIC is compounded in a patient suffering from OTC deficiency, because the blood clots weaken the liver still further, leading to a rapid increase in plasma levels of ammonia. Moreover, the only treatment for DIC is to deal with the underlying cause, the microbial infection; but in Gelsinger's case the infecting agent, the AD vector, was overpowering and impossible to treat directly. By Tuesday afternoon Gelsinger had slipped into a coma and was placed on blood dialysis to control the ammonia concentration that was rising to dangerous levels. His father arrived at the hospital early Wednesday morning and Drs. Raper and Batshaw told him they would have to put his son into a deeper coma in order to control the rising level of ammonia in his blood. Later that afternoon, Gelsinger's lungs and kidneys began to fail, and his body and face swelled to such an extent that he was barely recognizable. On the morning of Friday, September 17, Jesse Gelsinger was declared brain dead and he died at 2:30 P.M. that day.

The Investigation

Wilson reported Gelsinger's death immediately. Officials at FDA and NIH decided to terminate all AD vector gene therapy trials pending a full review of Gelsinger's case. A preliminary review was conducted from November 30, 1999, to January 19, 2000. The full review was to last for more than a year and covered every aspect of Wilson's protocol and the criteria used to admit patients to the trial. The investigation also examined the research labs at Genovo, a biotechnology company founded by Dr. Wilson, because it was there that much of the preclinical research was carried out. Genovo was also funding one-fifth of the operating budget for the Institute for Human Gene Therapy (IHGT), established by Wilson at the University of Pennsylvania, and in return Genovo had exclusive rights to patent and market any of IHGT's discoveries.

In January 2000 NIH released preliminary results of its investigation, which cited Wilson and Batshaw for failure to adhere to the clinical protocol and an apparent disregard for the safety of the study subjects. The report focused on four main points:

1. *Failure to adhere to the stopping rules.* Toxic reactions observed in cohorts 1 to 5 should have led to termination of the trial long before Gelsinger was treated. Many of the patients in these groups suffered harsher reactions to the treatment than was expected, and this should have been sufficient reason to stop the trial. In addition, most of the toxic reactions experienced by the patients in this study had never been reported to the FDA or NIH. In the months following Gelsinger's death, other investigations showed that failure to report toxic reactions was common in many gene therapy trials. In one study, the patients experienced 691 serious side effects, of which only 39 were reported as required by the federal agencies.

2. *Failure to adhere to the principle of informed consent.* When a toxic response occurred in cohort 1 of the Gelsinger trial, cohort 2 should have been informed of this response to give those patients the option of withdrawing from the study. This was not done. Moreover, the investigators discovered that none of the subjects were told about adverse effects on monkeys in the preclinical trial. One of the monkeys received the same virus used in the clinical trial, though at a proportionally higher dose, and within a week of being treated it was euthanized because it developed the same clotting disorder that killed Gelsinger. Since none of the subjects were told about this, the consent forms were ruled invalid.

3. *Failure to keep adequate records regarding vector lineage and titer.* This was an especially damaging finding since it implied that the researchers gave Gelsinger more virus than they thought they had. The term *titer* refers to the number of vector particles in a given solution. Determining the titer is not straightforward, and if errors are made, the concentration may be incorrect by a factor of 10,

rather than, say, double or triple the amount expected. The possibility that Gelsinger was accidentally given a higher-than-stated dose is suggested by the fact that a woman in his cohort received a nearly identical dose (3.0×10^{13}) without signs of liver damage or DIC. As already mentioned, a monkey in a preclinical trial received a higher dose (17 times greater) of the same virus and subsequently developed DIC. If researchers made an error in calculating the dose for Gelsinger, it is possible he received an equivalent, fatal amount.

4. *Changing the protocol without approval.* The most serious infraction here had to do with the ammonia levels in the blood of prospective volunteers. As laid out in the original protocol, patients having more than 50 micromoles of ammonia per milliliter of blood were barred from volunteering because such a test result indicates severe liver damage. Sometime after the trial, however, researchers increased this maximum to 70 micromoles without formal approval from the FDA. Gelsinger's ammonia level on the day he was treated was about 60 micromoles. If the original cutoff had been adhered to, he would have been excluded from the study. However, in fairness to Wilson's team, it should be noted that ammonia levels fluctuate on a daily basis, and previous tests of Gelsinger's blood showed it to be less than 50 micromoles.

Concluding Remarks

The death of Jesse Gelsinger had the same effect on the gene therapy community that the *Columbia* disaster of 2003 had on NASA's space program. In both cases the initial shock and trauma, particularly for the families of those that died, was followed by a determined and unrelenting investigation that clarified the many events leading up to the accident and, at the same time, produced a clear picture of what had to be done to ensure that such terrible accidents never happen again.

Many things were changed at NASA to help shake the program administrators out of their complacency and to open their eyes to the real dangers of each space shuttle mission. Similarly, the gene therapy community had begun to think the procedure was so safe and straightforward that they were lulled into complacency, and in the case of the

OTC trial, researchers ignored warning signs that could have prevented both Gelsinger's death and the severe illnesses other members of the trial developed.

In March 2000, after the completion of their investigation of the Gelsinger trial, the FDA and NIH announced a set of new initiatives to protect participants in gene therapy trials. The main thrust of the new guidelines is a monitoring plan that requires strict adherence, on the part of the investigators, to report, within seven days, any and all toxic effects. All such reports are now reviewed by an independent data and safety monitoring board before the trial is allowed to continue. To ensure compliance, NIH investigators now make frequent unannounced visits to the institutions where gene therapy trials are being conducted. The new initiatives also require full disclosure of preclinical data to potential volunteers before they sign the consent form. Consistent with this goal is a new database at the NIH Web site that provides public access to detailed information concerning NIH-funded gene therapy trials. The FDA has established a similar public access point for this kind of information with its Gene Therapy Patient Tracking System, established in June 2002, and made available on its Web site.

Even in the darkest hours immediately following the death of Jesse Gelsinger, no one believed it would be the end of gene therapy, any more than the destruction of the shuttle *Columbia* (or the previous explosion of the shuttle *Challenger* in 1986) was thought to signal the end of the space program. In the case of gene therapy, science offers cures for a wide variety of noxious diseases that have plagued humans for centuries. With the new regulations in place and safer procedures being developed, scientists will continue their efforts to realize its full potential.

·5·

FUTURE PROSPECTS

Gene therapy has had its ups and downs. Indeed, more than any other new biology technology, this one is the most erratic. It had great success with the DeSilva case but a terrible failure with the Gelsinger case. Even worse, in 2002 a French trial to cure SCIDs, led by Dr. Alain Fischer and initially thought to be the most successful ever, suffered a setback when two of the participants developed a vector-induced leukemia.

The trouble besetting the Fischer trial does not mark the end of gene therapy, but it has helped scientists define the problems that must be resolved in order to improve the safety of this procedure: Safer vehicles must be found or designed, strategies must be developed to minimize immune rejection of the vector, and greater emphasis must be placed on risk assessment. The last of these three problem areas will be relatively easy to achieve, but the first two represent profoundly difficult biological problems that are likely to take many years to resolve.

Safer Vehicles

A safe vehicle is one that enters only the target cells and inserts itself into a safe location within the genome—that is, well away from any genes. Retroviruses, for reasons outlined in chapter 2, are the vector of choice for most gene therapy trials, but none of them are capable of this kind of specificity. The failure of the Fischer trial, which used a modified retrovirus (MuLV), occurred because the vector inserted itself into a stretch of DNA in or near a gene called *LMO2* that is known to be involved in cancer induction, particularly leukemias.

Scientists have estimated that the MuLV vector, used in the Fischer trial, could have inserted itself in the *LMO2* gene in one in 100,000 cells. Each patient in the trial received about 1 million genetically modified cells, so it is likely that some of the patients received at least one cell containing a vector-mutated *LMO2* gene. However, this estimate is based on the assumption that vector insertion is random, which may not always be the case. Some viruses may insert themselves nonrandomly into preferred sites within the genome. In this way, a leukemia virus such as MuLV may habitually insert itself in or near genes that cause cancer, in which case the number of cells damaged in the Fischer trial may have been much higher than one in 100,000. Consequently, a virus such as MuLV may never be a safe vehicle. Nonrandom insertion poses a serious threat to virus-based gene therapy, but it also suggests a way of improving the safety of all insertional vectors, for if they are nonrandom, there may be a way of designing a vector that will insert itself only into specific areas of the genome. (See the gene therapy updates in chapter 8 for additional information.)

SEQUENCE-SPECIFIC VECTOR INSERTION

Insertion of viral DNA into the chromosome is regulated by a viral protein called an integrase. During the life cycle of a retrovirus, the conversion of the RNA genome into DNA is followed by the translocation of the viral DNA into the cell's nucleus, where it is transcribed into messenger RNAs (mRNAs). The viral mRNAs move out to the cytoplasm where they are translated into protein. Integrase is among this group of viral proteins; because it carries a nuclear localization signal, cellular enzymes escort it back into the nucleus, where it catalyzes the insertion of viral DNA into host chromosomes. The details of this event involve the binding of the integrase to the viral DNA, cutting of the host DNA by the integrase, and finally, insertion of the viral DNA into the cell's chromosome. Thus, it is the integrase that decides where the viral DNA will be inserted. It is this protein, and others like it, that will make sequence-specific insertion possible.

The year 2003 saw the completion of the human genome project, an effort that has given the world the complete nucleotide sequence of the human genome. With this information at hand, scientists will be able to map out the exact location of all human genes and the noncoding

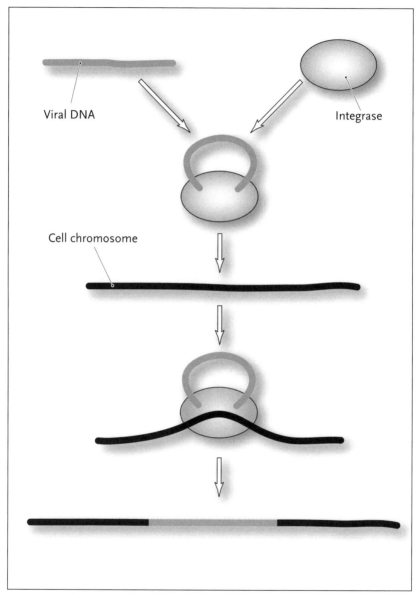

Integration of viral DNA into a cellular chromosome. The protein integrase binds to the viral DNA and then to the cellular chromosome (target), after which it cuts the target chromosome in a single place and inserts the viral DNA. Final sealing of the target and viral DNA is left to the cell's repair enzymes (not shown). The length of the viral DNA, relative to the cell chromosome, is exaggerated for clarity.

regions. Careful analysis of this data will make it possible to design a family of integrase molecules that will place a vector in a noncoding region of the genome. Indeed, it may be possible to map out entire genetic neighborhoods that could be designated as safe insertional sites, that all gene therapists could use without fear of damaging cellular genes. This approach will give gene therapy the kind of rational foundation that it lacks today.

IMPROVED TARGETING OF CELLS AND ORGANS

The most successful gene therapy trial to date is still the very first one: the DeSilva trial. The success of this trial is largely due to the fact that the target cells were lymphocytes, cells that could be easily isolated and removed from the blood, transformed with the corrected gene, and then returned to the patient's circulatory system. There is no targeting problem here, and while other things can still go wrong, as the Fischer trial demonstrated, the gene therapists know that the vector carrying the therapeutic gene is restricted to a single cell type.

This was not the case with the Gelsinger trial. Liver cells cannot be harvested, transformed, and then returned to the patient. Instead, the vector had to be injected into the body, after which the physicians crossed their fingers and hoped that most of it ended up in liver cells and not everywhere else in the body. The scientists conducting the Gelsinger trial took special precautions to ensure that the vector remained in the liver, but it did not. The virus spilled out into general circulation where it entered many different kinds of cells throughout Gelsinger's body, with disastrous consequences. But if a vector is safe, and designed to insert itself away from cellular genes, does it really matter if it enters a single cell type versus many? Were it not for the patient's immune system, the answer to this question would be no. But the immune system will try to kill any cells that are infected with the vector. The infected cell in effect signs its own death warrant by displaying vector antigens on its surface. Lymphocytes detect these foreign antigens and either kill the cell directly or force it to commit suicide. This system is essential for fighting infectious diseases, but it does not understand the difference between a gene therapy vector and an influenza virus. Consequently, gene therapy must be designed to minimize the number of cell types that will become infected with the vector. If the vector does stimulate an immune response then physicians have to deal with only the possible failure of a single organ, versus the multiorgan failure that killed Jesse Gelsinger.

Improved targeting requires matching either viral capsid proteins, such as the retroviral gp 120 (see figure on page 21), or the adenovirus fiber proteins (see figure on page 18) to cell-surface receptors. A hypo-

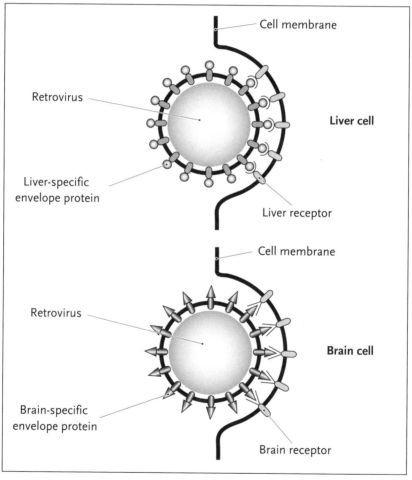

Vector targeting for safer gene therapy. Greater safety can be achieved by designing vectors that have cell-specific envelope proteins. In this way, for instance, brain-specific vectors would not be able to enter liver cells and, likewise, liver-specific vectors would be blocked from entering brain cells.

thetical matching scheme using a retrovirus is shown in the figure on page 60. Accomplishing such a matching scheme will be extremely difficult, as it requires detailed sequence information for both the viral proteins and the cell surface receptors. Some of this information is currently available for the vectors, and with the human sequence data now available, reliable targeting will likely be available for gene therapy trials in the next five to 10 years.

Reducing Immune Rejection of the Vector

Gene therapy trials that target the cells of solid organs require injection of the vehicle into general circulation. This is analogous to throwing a sheep into a den of very hungry wolves. Immune system sentinels (described in chapter 3) begin an immediate attack on the invader, and their pursuit is relentless. Most of the vector particles will never make it to the target cells, and those that do may end up being destroyed by natural killer cells along with any cells they have entered. It is not surprising, therefore, that the efficiency of gene therapy is extremely low, often too low to be of therapeutic benefit. Thus, gene therapists face challenges that are identical to those arising from organ transplantations. Both have to negotiate with the patient's immune system, or there is no hope of success. For gene therapists, as for transplant surgeons, there are only two ways to deal with the immune system: Give the patient immunosuppressants to deactivate the system, or camouflage the vector in some way to make it invisible, or at least acceptable, to the lymphocytes and other members of the immune system.

IMMUNOSUPPRESSANTS

Two drugs commonly used for organ transplants are cyclosporine and tacrolimus. Both of these compounds are isolated from fungus and exert their effect by blocking the adaptive immune response, thus inactivating recruitment of T lymphocytes and natural killer cells by the monocytes. One or both of these drugs could be given to a patient immediately before the vector is administered and then slowly withdrawn once it has entered the target cells. However, to date, immunosuppressants have not been used but are under study for inclusion in future gene therapy trials.

VECTOR CAMOUFLAGE

Artificial vectors, consisting of a phospholipid sphere called a liposome, have been designed in the hope of camouflaging the vector from the immune system. The immune system is on guard against foreign glycoproteins and glycolipids, components of a typical glycocalyx, the molecular forest that covers the surface of every cell. From the lymphocyte's point of view, evaluating a glycocalyx is rather like being an ecologist flying over an Earth forest and getting a general impression of the for-

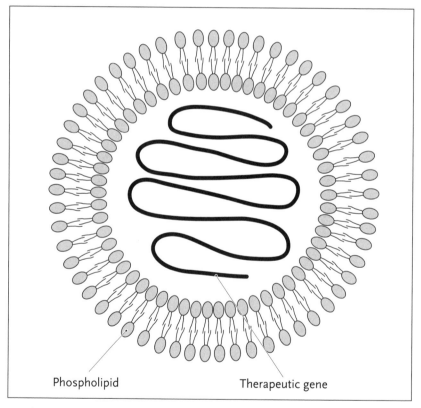

Phospholipid   Therapeutic gene

Lipid vectors. Artificial vectors can be made for gene therapy by encasing the therapeutic gene inside a bubble called a liposome, consisting of a phospholipid bilayer (shown in cross-section). Lipid vectors have the advantage of not being attacked by the immune system. On the other hand, they lack targeting specificity and will enter virtually every cell in the body.

est's identity and health, by noting the kinds and variety of trees that are present. In this sense an Earth forest is an ecological fingerprint. In the world of immunology, the glycocalyx is a cellular fingerprint. Lymphocytes are programmed to know which fingerprints represent a normal part of the body, and those that fail to register as self are marked as foreign and dealt with accordingly.

Phospholipids, the base material for prokaryote and eukaryote cell membranes, are not deemed a threat by the immune system; consequently, a liposome can move through the circulatory system unmolested. The great disadvantage of lipid vectors is their lack of target specificity. A liposome can readily diffuse across any cell membrane, and, if there are enough of them, will enter every cell in the body. As previously explained, a viral vector entering most or all of the cells in the body can lead to a fatal multiorgan failure as the immune system destroys the infected cells. With liposomes, there is no danger of viral antigens being displayed on the membrane of infected cells, but the lack of targeting specificity is a problem for other reasons: First, the therapeutic gene will be expressed in nontarget cells. Disregarding the wastefulness of this result, there is no telling what effect the gene may have in an inappropriate cellular environment. Second, since the vector is entering many cells, its effects on the target cells will be diluted and therefore diminished. Gene therapists try to maximize the amount of the therapeutic gene that enters the target cells so the therapy has a chance of doing some good. Gene therapy trials often fail because too little of the vector gets into too few of the target cells, and although the gene is expressed in those cells, it is too little to relieve the patient's symptoms.

Nevertheless, lipid vectors have great potential and it may be possible to improve targeting specificity by embedding proteins in the bilayer that will bind to cell-specific receptors, while at the same time being acceptable to the immune system. Most work with lipid vectors is at the initial stage of development, being tested primarily in mice and rats. Routine use of these vectors in human trials is not expected until 2005.

Improved Risk Assessment

In their report following the death of Jesse Gelsinger, NIH focused extensively on the issue of risk assessment, particularly regarding the detection and reporting of toxic reactions experienced by the patients in the Gelsinger clinical trial. NIH investigators noted that most of the toxic reactions experienced by the patients in that study were never reported to FDA or NIH, and that follow-up investigations concluded that failure to report toxic reactions was common in many gene therapy trials. In one study (cited in chapter 4), the patients experienced 691 serious side effects; of these, only 39 were reported as required by the federal agencies.

Legal guidelines are now in place to force investigators to report toxic reactions. The problem is determining the parameters that are to be tested and the cutoff point that separates a benign response from a toxic reaction. Important elements of good risk assessment include the following: initial vector titer and subsequent vector concentration in the patients' blood, vector insertion and proliferation, and the response status of the immune system. Jesse Gelsinger may have died simply because the initial vector titer (the number of viral particles per milliliter) of the solution injected into his liver was too high. Obvious errors such as this occur more frequently than scientists like to admit, but can be minimized by a three-tiered evaluation protocol (that is, three independent determinations of the titer).

As already pointed out, future vectors will be designed to insert at specific places within the genome. But a vector designed for improved targeting cannot be trusted to do what it is programmed to do. Tests must be incorporated into a standard gene therapy protocol that determines the actual insertion site of the vector, and if it is not where it is supposed to be, steps must be taken to deal with the possible side effects. These evaluations pertain to any evidence that suggests the virus is replicating. Most viruses used for gene therapy are altered so they cannot replicate, but it is always possible that the vector will encounter a wild virus that is already infecting the patient, and that the two will recombine genetically to produce a replication-competent vector. Research is also under way to improve targeting of cells and organs. Clinical trials must include tests to confirm the targeting of these vectors, and if vectors enter a variety of nontarget cells, such information should be taken as involving a potential toxic response.

The final area of risk assessment, involving the immune system response, is the easiest to evaluate, yet provides the most important information. It was, after all, the response of Gelsinger's immune system that proved fatal. An increasing white blood cell count after vector administration, coupled with high vector titer, is a deadly mix, and it must be the focus of any attempt to improve the safety of gene therapy.

Redesigning Human Anatomy and Physiology

With the human genome now completely sequenced and researchers actively seeking ways to move genes in and out of cell nuclei, it will soon be possible to modify our physiology, not just for the purpose of fighting disease, but in an attempt to change the way the body functions, and even to change the way it looks. These applications are fundamentally different from attempts to correct a medical disorder in that they could change the basic nature of human beings rather than reestablishing normal functions. Indeed, once gene therapy matures, there will be no limit to the kinds of things that it can do to our cellular and physiological systems. The possibilities may be grouped into three kinds of gene therapy: physiological, cosmetic, and bizarre. Ethical and legal questions regarding the future applications of gene therapy will be left to following chapters.

PHYSIOLOGICAL GENE THERAPY

It takes more than carbon-based organic compounds to run a human being. Inorganic salts such as sodium chloride, potassium chloride, and calcium chloride play important roles in our physiology. Metals such as iron and copper also have a role to play. Indeed, without these metals we would suffocate for lack of oxygen, or fall into a deep coma for lack of ATP, the energy carrier that is vital to the survival of every cell in the body. ATP is produced in a two-step process involving a number of metal-binding proteins called the respiratory chain (also known as the electron transport chain) and a special ion channel-enzyme called ATP synthetase. The respiratory chain consists of three major components: NADH dehydrogenase, cytochrome b, and cytochrome oxidase. All of these components are protein complexes that have an iron (in the case of NADH dehydrogenase and cytochrome b) or a copper core (cytochrome oxidase), together with the ATP synthetase located in the inner membrane of the mitochondria.

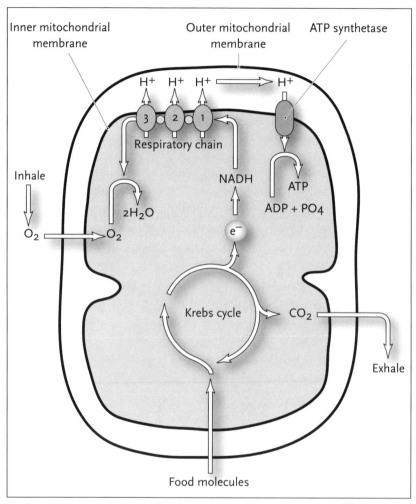

Production of ATP by mitochondria. Food molecules are processed through the citric acid cycle to produce electrons (e⁻) that are stored in NADH. The respiratory chain consists of three major components: NADH dehydrogenase, cytochrome b, and cytochrome oxidase. The first component in the chain captures the stored electrons by separating NADH into NAD and H⁺ (not shown). The electrons travel through the chain powering a pumping function of each component, resulting in a proton (H⁺) concentration gradient across the inner membrane, and are eventually transferred to oxygen (O_2) leading to the production of water. The protons, moving down their concentration gradient, power the synthesis of ATP by the synthetase. The only exhaust from this power plant is water, which the cell uses, and CO_2, a gas that is exhaled by the lungs.

The respiratory chain is analogous to an electric cable that transports electricity from a hydroelectric dam to our homes, where it is used to turn on lights or to power a stereo. The human body, like that of all animals, generates electricity by processing food molecules through a metabolic pathway called the Krebs cycle. The electricity, or electrons so generated, are not released as free particles, but are transferred to a hydrogen ion (H^+), which quickly binds to nicotinamide adenine dinucleotide (NAD). Binding of the hydrogen ion to NAD is noted by abbreviating the resulting molecule as NADH. The electrons begin their journey down the respiratory chain when NADH binds to NADH dehydrogenase, the first component in the chain. This enzyme does just what its name implies: It removes the hydrogen from NADH, releasing the stored electrons, which are conducted through the chain by the iron and copper, as though they were traveling along an electrical wire. All electrical circuits must have a ground; that is, the electrons need someplace to go once they have completed the circuit. In the case of the respiratory chain, the ground is oxygen. After passing through cytochrome oxidase, the last component in the chain, the electrons are picked up by oxygen, which combines with hydrogen ions to form water. As the electrons travel from one end of the chain to the other they energize an ion-pumping function of each protein complex, leading to the movement of hydrogen ions (H^+) across the inner membrane (the same H^+ produced when NADH dehydrogenase releases the electrons by separating NADH into NAD and H^+). The H^+ passes through the ATP synthetase and thereby energizes the synthesis of ATP from ADP and inorganic phosphate (P_i).

The respiratory chain is a complex system that plays a crucial role in the formation of ATP. A central feature of this system is the use of iron and copper to provide electric power to the three ion-pumping stations that are part of the chain. This system was originated by prokaryotes at least 2 billion years ago, and it provides a highly efficient method for extracting energy from the food we eat. Yet despite its ingenuity, it is not necessarily the best design possible, for there are other metals, such as gold and silver, that are much better electrical conductors than are iron or copper. But we cannot blame the prokaryotes for this; they designed the respiratory chain around iron and copper simply because those metals were much more abundant than gold or silver. The fact that the respiratory chain is iron- and copper-based is simply an artifact of Earth's geology. Likewise, human electricians use copper wires, not gold or silver wires, simply because copper is readily available and very cheap.

Because gold and silver are nearly 10 times better at conducting electricity than copper or iron, we can expect that a respiratory chain based on gold and silver would be much more efficient than the one we now have, being able to produce a much greater quantity of ATP in a shorter period of time. This would have the effect of postponing the onset of fatigue, perhaps indefinitely. With gene therapy, the prospect of converting human physiology to a gold- and silver-based respiratory chain is within the realm of possibility. This would require a detailed analysis of the proteins making up the major components of the chain so they may be modified to enhance their binding to gold and silver, rather than copper and iron. Once such an analysis was done, the genes could be designed to code for these proteins, after which they would be introduced into human cells.

The respiratory chain is not the only major system that may someday be modified by gene therapy. As mentioned, the ground for the electrons passing through the respiratory chain is oxygen, a gas in the air we breathe. The oxygen is picked up in our lungs by hemoglobin, another iron-binding protein complex. All vertebrates use hemoglobin, but many invertebrates, such as crabs and lobsters, prefer a copper-binding protein called hemocyanin. Hemocyanin has an advantage over hemoglobin that explorers and future astronauts may find compelling: It has a higher affinity for oxygen and therefore is well suited for environments that have a low oxygen content, such as high altitudes or the surface of other planets. The substitution of hemocyanin for hemoglobin in humans would be much simpler than renovating the respiratory chain. This is because the protein already exists and the hemocyanin gene has been isolated from invertebrates. The hemocyanin gene could be inserted into human cells and both the old and new genes designed in such a way that they could be turned on or off at will depending on the need. An astronaut visiting an oxygen-depleted world could turn off the hemoglobin gene, turn on the hemocyanin gene, and then switch back once the mission was completed.

Swapping metal ions, in blood pigments or the respiratory chain, would have profound effects on our physiology. Indeed, these simple differences in the metallic content of crucial proteins based on local geology, are likely to be the source of major differences between the people of Earth and creatures (if any) that evolved on other planets. Aside from functional differences, these changes would also affect an individual's appearance. Human skin tone (aside from melanin coloring) is determined by the iron in our blood and in the respiratory chain. Substitute hemoglobin for hemocyanin and the blood becomes pale blue (the color of crab blood); substitute copper and iron in the respiratory system for gold and silver, and our skin tone would likely shift to a pale golden hue.

Some scientists have speculated about the possibility of using gene therapy to improve our intelligence, to reverse the aging process, and even to dampen aggressive behavior. However, these would be extremely difficult tasks to accomplish. The main problem here is that intelligence, aging and behavior are controlled by many genes, none of which have so far been identified. But even if they were, it is difficult enough to manage single-gene therapy, let alone trying to insert a dozen or more genes in their proper place and have them all function according to plan. Successful single-gene therapy is still 10 to 20 years into the future, and multigene therapy to influence complex physiological processes will not even be approachable for many years beyond that.

COSMETIC GENE THERAPY

Skin color, eye color, hair color, baldness, height, and weight are all physical characteristics that could be modified with gene therapy. Giant fish have already been produced by introducing extra copies of the growth hormone (GH) gene that stimulates bone and muscle growth. Parents who want their children to be really big could have them injected with a GH-vector soon after birth, or anytime before they enter puberty, in order to maximize their size. They could also elect to have their children injected with a melanin-stimulating or melanin-inhibiting vector depending on whether they want their children's skin to be dark or light. Hair and eye color could be controlled just as easily by substituting the child's natural color genes with others of their choice.

Of course, adults may also want to make similar changes to themselves. Baldness is a condition that many men, and a few women, would choose to treat with gene therapy. There would be no contest between this approach and hair implants or the use of a wig. Hair dyeing is another cosmetic alteration that is commonly performed by adults. Gene therapy could permanently restore the hair's natural color or make it a different color altogether.

None of the cosmetic applications of gene therapy are currently available owing to the danger of the procedure. However, the cosmetics industry will likely bring these applications to market as soon as a safe delivery system is available. Whether people will subject themselves, or be allowed to subject their children, to physiological or cosmetic gene therapy will be discussed in the next chapter.

BIZARRE GENE THERAPY

How bizarre could gene therapy become? Could ancient myths of wizards and witches casting spells on people to turn them into frogs or monsters become a reality? Does gene therapy have the potential for such gross changes to our physical characteristics?

If we can use gene therapy to treat baldness, we can use it to grow hair over an entire body. Add in a gene to stimulate the growth of canine teeth, and a human could easily be converted into something right out of *Beauty and the Beast*. If we can use gene therapy to darken or lighten our skin, we could also use it to make someone's skin bright red, or green, or any color for which a gene has been isolated. And if we can use gene therapy to modify our weight, we could also use it to make people really fat or extremely thin. Opening our genome to the whole world, and then providing that world with a technology for accessing and altering the information contained therein, is a very risky business. No one knows how it will play out. The danger to society could be unleashed intentionally or accidentally. For instance, a research lab working on a vector to grow hair could suffer a breach in its containment facility, leading to widespread infection of a local community, with possibly devastating consequences. Or bioterrorists might devise a vector that coded for a chemical that could render people unconscious within a few hours. Viewed in this way, the future of gene therapy could hold perils that far exceed the threat of conventional germ warfare.

.6.

ETHICS OF
GENE THERAPY

The ethical problems associated with gene therapy are the same as those pertaining to any biomedical research that uses humans as experimental subjects. The development of a code of ethics governing these situations can be traced back to the Nuremberg trials, which convened immediately after World War II to prosecute Nazi war criminals. In the course of those trials, evidence was presented regarding the use of prisoners in the concentration camps as "research subjects." As a consequence, the Nuremberg code of ethics was formalized, and was later expanded on by the Belmont Report, produced in the United States, to address a severe breach in research ethics that surfaced in Tuskegee, Alabama, in 1972.

The Belmont Report

In 1932 a research institute in Tuskegee, Alabama, enrolled 600 low-income African-American males in a study dealing with the progression of syphilis. These patients, 400 of whom were already infected with syphilis, were monitored for 40 years. The infected individuals were never told they had syphilis, but instead were told that their medical problems were due to "bad blood." In 1947 penicillin became widely available and was known throughout the medical world as an effective treatment for syphilis, yet the participants in the Tuskegee study were never told there was an antibiotic available that could cure them. The study was terminated in 1972 by the U.S. Department of Health, only when its existence was leaked to the general public, and it became a political embarrassment. By the time the study was terminated, 28 of the men had died of syphilis, 100 others were dead from related complications, 40 of the participants' wives had been infected, and 19 children had contracted the disease at birth. Public revulsion over the details of this study was instrumental in forcing the government to introduce new policies and laws regarding the use of human subjects in medical research.

On July 12, 1975, the National Research Act was signed into law, creating a national commission to protect human research subjects. This commission was charged with the task of identifying basic ethical principles that should govern the conduct of any research involving human subjects; in February 1976 the commission produced the Belmont Report (so named because the report was finalized at the Smithsonian Institute's Belmont Conference Center). The report began by defining three basic ethical principles that should be applied to research involving human subjects: respect for persons, beneficence, and justice.

RESPECT FOR PERSONS Respect for persons demands that subjects enter into research voluntarily and with adequate information. This assumes the individuals are autonomous agents— that is, they are competent to make up their own minds. However, there are many instances in which potential research subjects are not really autonomous: prisoners, patients in a mental institution, children, the elderly, and the infirm. All of these people require special protection to ensure they are not being coerced or fooled into volunteering as research subjects. The subjects in the Tuskegee study were all poor, uneducated farmworkers who were especially vulnerable to coercion.

BENEFICENCE It is not enough to respect potential subjects' decisions and to protect them from harm. In addition, it is necessary to do all that is possible to ensure their well-being. Beneficence is generally regarded as acts of kindness or charity, but the report insisted that it be made an obligation in the case of research subjects. In this sense it is the natural extension of the Hippocratic oath that all physicians are expected to adhere by: *I will give no deadly medicine to anyone if asked, nor suggest any such counsel.* In other words, the doctor must do no harm. For those involved in biomedical research, this means never injuring one person to benefit another.

JUSTICE   Those volunteering to be research subjects should, if at all possible, reap some of the benefits. This is a question of justice, in the sense of fairness of distribution. The exploitation of prisoners in Nazi concentration camps may have produced results that could benefit the Nazis but certainly did not benefit the people they experimented on. The Tuskegee study used disadvantaged rural black men to study the untreated course of a disease that is by no means restricted to that population.

Guided by these three ethical principles, the Belmont Report introduced the following requirements that all human research trials must adhere to: informed consent, risk/benefit assessment, and fair selection of research subjects.

INFORMED CONSENT   All participants must provide informed consent in writing. Moreover, steps must be taken to ensure the consent is, in fact, informed. This might involve an independent assessment of the individual's ability to understand the language on the consent form and any instructions or explanations the investigators have given. Since the Gelsinger trial, this process has been amended to include a patient advocate who is present at any meeting between the physicians and the prospective volunteers. This approach has the added advantage of ensuring that scientists do not give prospective subjects misleading or inaccurate information or try to coerce them in any way.

RISK/BENEFIT ASSESSMENT   There is no point in having an ethical standard based on doing no harm if there is no formalized method available for assessing the risk to a patient. It is the risk that is paramount in a patient's mind. No matter how grand the possible benefits, few would volunteer if they thought they would die as a consequence. The only exception to this might be terminally ill patients who volunteer for a clinical trial, even though they know they are not likely to survive it. Independent committees monitor risk assessment based on information supplied by the investigators. In general, risks should be reduced to those necessary to achieve the research objective. If there is significant risk, review committees are expected to demand a justification for it.

SELECTION OF SUBJECTS   The selection process must be fair. Low-risk, potentially beneficial research should not be offered to one segment of society, nor should high-risk research be limited to prisoners, low-income groups, or anyone in a disadvantaged social position.

CONCLUSIONS   The Belmont Report introduced the principle of informed consent. Backing this up is the recommendation for independent review committees that ensure the ethical guidelines are being followed. In the United States the FDA and NIH are responsible for enforcing the guidelines laid out by the Belmont Report. In addition, there are local review committees called institutional review boards that must approve any experimentation using human subjects. The Belmont Report was inspired by the general public's anger over the Tuskegee study, so it is fitting that on May 16, 1997, the surviving members of the Tuskegee study were invited to the White House, where President Bill Clinton issued a formal apology and reaffirmed the nation's commitment to rigorous ethical standards in biomedical research to ensure that such flagrant abuses of basic human rights would never happen again. No one would have believed, at the time, that further trouble was just around the corner.

Clinical Trials

The investigation into the Gelsinger trial concluded just three years after President Clinton's apology to the Tuskegee patients. While the abuses in this later trial are not as serious, they are of a similar kind. The investigation (described in chapter 2) charged the researchers with essentially four violations: 1) failure to adhere to stopping rules, 2) failure to adhere to the principle of informed consent, 3) failure to keep adequate records, and 4) changing the protocol without approval. Of these charges, the first and second are clear violations of even the most basic of ethical standards.

The principle of informed consent is central to society's acceptance of the use of humans as experimental animals. However, there is a tendency for some people in both the science community and the general public to think of clinical trials as routine medical procedures. They are not. Clinical trials are experiments, and while scientists may claim confidence in the outcome, they really do not know how things will work out; that is, after all, the basic nature of the research process. To give the public, or the research subjects, any other impression is unethical. That being the case, there can be no excuse for any deviation from the principle of informed consent. Any patient will give consent to an experimental therapy if he or she expects to be cured, or at least no worse off. All the participants in the Gelsinger trial believed that the worst side effect of the treatment would be a cold or a flu. The researchers did not tell them about the prior death of a monkey treated with a similar protocol, nor did they make it clear to the prospective patients that they might suffer excessive fever or organ damage. Even when some of the patients in the study began to develop these symptoms, the researchers did not tell the other members of the study, thus failing again to adhere to the basic intent of informed consent.

Failure to adhere to the stopping rules is, in a sense, another failure of informed consent; had the investigators stopped one cohort, it would have been a signal to the other cohorts, and to the NIH, that something was wrong. Failure to abide by their own protocol suggests the possibility that the researchers included the safeguards only to get federal approval for the study, not to protect the health and interests of their human subjects.

An important lesson to be learned from the Gelsinger trial is that scientists involved in clinical trials cannot be trusted to act ethically as long as they have a financial stake in the outcome. Wilson's company funded much of the research leading up to the trial and, by taking out a patent on the vector design, stood to earn a great deal of money if the procedure worked. This question of the investigator's financial stake in the outcome applies to a great many procedures in biomedical research, including stem cell research, animal cloning, and even clinical trials testing artificial hearts. In practice, a clear separation between the investigators and the possibility of personal financial gain will be almost impossible to guarantee, simply because so many clinical trials are dependent on biotech or pharmaceutical companies for funding. Consequently, the general public will have to put its faith in federal agencies, such as FDA and NIH, to develop enforceable guidelines for gene therapy trials—and indeed for all medical research trials—so everyone involved will have a clear idea of what is going on, who stands to profit by it, and what the risks are.

Physiological Enhancement

It is almost certain that gene therapy in the future will not be restricted to curing diseases but will also be used to enhance our physiology. Procedures to alter to our basic physiology could come from the medical community or privately owned pharmaceutical and biotech companies. Although the medical profession is primarily concerned with curing diseases, it also provides a great range of surgical procedures that are essentially cosmetic in nature. Patients who want to change the shape of their noses (rhinoplasty) or faces are not confronted with an ethical dilemma. In such cases, the only problem to work out is the question of who pays the bill. Medical insurance companies generally refuse to pay for elective or cosmetic surgery, so payment is the patient's responsibility.

However, physiological enhancement has the potential for serious ethical problems depending on the details of the procedure and whether it is to be done on a consenting adult or on a child. Rhinoplasty is usually performed on adults, and while the operation changes their appearance, it does not change their genotype. That is, whatever changes are made, they cannot be passed on to successive generations. This may not be the case with a gene therapy trial to alter the respiratory chain or to introduce extra copies of the GH gene. Even with refined vectors, there is always the possibility the change will affect the gonads, thus altering the individual's germ line. If that happens, the children of those gene therapy subjects stand a chance of inheriting an altered physiology.

The practice of altering human physiology, particularly if it involves the germ line, introduces serious ethical and moral problems, because it presupposes an understanding of nature that we do not possess and are not likely to possess in the foreseeable future. By conducting such experiments, we remove our evolution from the guidance of natural selection and place it squarely in the hands of a few scientists and technicians who think they know what is best for the future development of our species. Local prejudices and shortsightedness are almost certain to prevail, with the final product being a relatively homogeneous human population, ill-equipped to deal with the realities of the natural world. This situation is equivalent to the genetic bottlenecks that happen occasionally in the natural world. One example is the cheetah, an animal that neared extinction about 100,000 years ago, leaving only a few individuals to reestablish the population. All cheetahs alive today are very closely related; this could be a fatal problem if an unusually virulent bacterial or viral strain ever infects these animals. Human populations have been hit with many such epidemics through the ages, but it was our genetic diversity that provided the crucial immunity for large numbers of individuals. Tinkering with our genetic heritage at our current stage of development might improve our lot, but it is just as likely to drive us to the brink of extinction.

Cosmetic Applications

The caveats associated with the use of gene therapy for cosmetic purposes are to ensure that it is being done on consenting adults and that the vector will not infect the germ line. But there is a tendency already afoot among some parents who want to alter the appearance of their children. Today this impulse plays out with the use of GH injections (not gene therapy) to influence the child's size. Gene therapy simply places more options on the shelf, such as skin and eye color, among others mentioned previously. Children cannot give informed consent, so is it ethical to subject them to these procedures?

Cosmetic applications require careful thought on the part of the medical community or the companies that are offering the treatment. How far should a prospective patient be allowed to go with cosmetic gene therapy? Should consenting adults be allowed to turn their skin bright red or blue if they want to? A current corollary to this problem is the availability of sex-change operations. Is the medical profession adopting an ethical stance by offering such operations, or is it simply catering to the delusions of people who may be better served by a psychiatrist rather than a surgeon?

The search for a cosmetic fix is usually framed in the context of personal freedom, and as long as the treatment is confined to a single individual there is no harm in it. But the use of gene therapy places the question on a different level, simply because of the possible risk of germ line damage or alteration. Ethicists tend to view the germ line as something that belongs to everyone, to the human species, and not to any one individual. Thus, each individual has a responsibility to protect that legacy. This is a concern that society needs to come to grips with now, before the full force of gene therapy becomes a reality.

·7·
LEGAL ISSUES

Gene therapy originated in the United States, primarily through the tireless efforts of Dr. W. French Anderson, who at the time was a research scientist at the National Institutes of Health (NIH), in Bethesda, Maryland, the location of the first gene therapy clinical trial (the DeSilva trial). Thus it was that governmental agencies in the United States were the first to deal with the legal issues associated with gene therapy. The manner by which they resolved these issues will be the focus of this chapter.

Legislation and regulation of gene therapy is complex and multi-layered, involving several U.S. government agencies and, in some cases, the courts. It is the nature of the procedure that has brought this about. Gene therapy involves a rival vector that is administered to a patient as though it were a drug, and so the ultimate regulation of the procedure falls to the Food and Drug Administration (FDA). Other agencies are involved in regulating this procedure by virtue of the fact that they provide financial support for the basic research and the clinical trial. Most gene therapy trials are funded by the NIH, which has special offices and committees that monitor the progress of all such trials to ensure they are conducted according to FDA regulations (see the table on page 81). In addition, patients involved in gene therapy trials or their families may resort to civil or criminal lawsuits in the event that something goes wrong, especially if it appears to be the fault of the treatment or errors on the part of the investigators. The Gelsinger legal trial will be described later in this chapter as an example of such a lawsuit.

Regulatory Agencies

FOOD AND DRUG ADMINISTRATION

The FDA is an agency within the Department of Health and Human Services and consists of eight centers and offices that deal with all aspects of food, drug, and radiological safety. The agency employs a staff of 9,000 with a network of 167 field offices. The FDA's mission is to promote and protect public health by getting safe and effective products to market as quickly as possible, and to continue monitoring product safety after they are in use. The FDA was formed in 1906 when Congress passed the Pure Food and Drug Act. The scope of the agency was expanded in 1936 with the passage of the Federal Food, Drug, and Cosmetic Act, giving it the power to ask the courts to issue injunctions or prosecute those that deliberately violate the agency's regulations.

In 1984 the FDA established the Center for Biologics Evaluation and Research (CBER), which has the responsibility of regulating gene therapy. In 1991 CBER issued a document that stipulated the precautions that must be taken in the manufacturing and testing of gene therapy products, thus broadening its scope to include all aspects of gene therapy, from product manufacturing to application in clinical trials. As defined by CBER, biologics, unlike the usual kinds of drugs, are derived from humans, animals, or microorganisms. Most biologics are complex mixtures that are not easily identified or characterized, and many of them are manufactured using biotechnology. In justifying their intent to regulate gene therapy, the FDA and CBER have made it clear that DNA or viral vectors that are administered to gene therapy patients are products that the agency has a mandate to regulate.

All gene therapy clinical trials require a license from the FDA, which monitors the progress of all trials through its Center for Biologics Evaluation and Research. Investigators must submit regular reports to the CBER, and in some cases, the center will conduct on-site inspections to ensure the trial is following the required guidelines. NIH-funded gene therapy trials are monitored by both the FDA and the NIH. The NIH monitoring effort is the responsibility of the Office of Biotechnology Activities, to which the RAC belongs, and the Office of Human Subjects Research. If officials at NIH discover a breach in regulations, they are

GENE THERAPY REGULATORY AGENCIES AND COMMITTEES IN THE UNITED STATES

Name	Abbreviation
Food and Drug Administration	FDA
Center for Biologics Evaluation and Research	CBER
National Institutes of Health	NIH
Office of Biotechnology Activities	OBA
Recombinant DNA Advisory Committee	RAC
Office of Human Subjects Research	OHSR

required by law to report it to the FDA, which has the ultimate power to terminate the trial and to order an investigation.

In 1993 the FDA released a guidance document that detailed the agency's legal basis for its regulation of gene therapy. The document explained that while the agency was created before the advent of gene therapies, its scope is sufficiently broad to encompass new and unexpected products that require testing and verification prior to marketing. The document defined gene therapy as a medical procedure based on genetic modification of living cells, and that the genetic manipulation is intended to treat disease or injuries in humans. According to the document, the products containing the genetic material, either DNA or a viral vector that is intended for gene therapy, are regulated as biological products (biologics) or as drugs. Consequently, gene therapy products require the premarket submission and approval of an application before they may be used in a clinical setting.

The investigator must also submit an Investigational New Drug application (IND) to the FDA demonstrating that the available preclinical (animal or laboratory) data justify testing the product on human subjects to see if it is safe and effective. The IND rules also require that the researcher has obtained approval from an institutional review board (IRB). Since the death of Jesse Gelsinger, in 1999, the FDA and NIH have announced new initiatives to protect participants in gene therapy trials. The FDA has suspended gene therapy trials at institutions the agency has found in violation of its requirements. FDA is currently monitoring more than 200 gene therapy trials, but has not as yet approved for sale any human gene therapy products.

NATIONAL INSTITUTES OF HEALTH

The NIH began as a one-room laboratory of hygiene in 1887 with an annual budget of $300. Since then, it has grown into one of the finest medical research centers in the world, with a staff of more than 18,000 and an annual budget that exceeded $27 billion in 2003. The mission of the NIH is the pursuit of fundamental knowledge of living systems and the application of that knowledge to the treatment of human diseases and disabilities. To that end, nearly 50,000 principal investigators at NIH laboratories and research centers throughout the country are funded by the NIH. The quality of NIH-funded research is of the highest caliber, with 106 of the grantees having been awarded the Nobel Prize as of 2004.

In 1974 the NIH established the Office of Biotechnology Activities (OBA), which formed the Recombinant DNA Advisory Committee (known as the RAC). This committee was given the responsibility of monitoring and regulating the newly discovered laboratory technique by which the DNA from different organisms could be recombined (termed "recombinant DNA") to form new, and potentially hazardous, hybrid molecules and organisms. Initially the RAC focused on safety concerns relating to the inadvertent release of recombinant DNA into the environment. In 1976 the RAC issued new regulations requiring institutions involved in recombinant DNA research to establish the Institutional Biohazard Committee for on-site regulation of such research.

In 1980 the OBA shifted its attention to the use of recombinant DNA in a newly devised procedure now known as gene therapy. In 1983 the RAC formed the Working Group on Human Gene Therapy, consisting of scientists, clinicians, lawyers, ethicists, policy experts, and public representatives. The Working Group recommended that the RAC broaden its scope to include a review of gene therapy protocols, and provided a list of questions and conditions that gene therapists must address in submissions to the RAC. All gene therapy protocols that are funded by NIH or conducted at NIH-funded institutions must be submitted to the RAC for approval. However, implementation of the protocol within the context of a clinical trial cannot proceed without the prior approval of the FDA. Thus, both organizations assume the responsibility of monitoring NIH-funded trials. Gene therapy trials that are not funded by NIH (that is, trials that are funded by biotech or pharmaceutical companies) require only the approval of the FDA, which takes full responsibility for subsequent monitoring and regulation. The great advantage of NIH-funded gene therapy research, from the point of view of the public's safety and concern, is that the review process and the monitoring are made public. Indeed, since the death of Jesse Gelsinger, NIH regulations have been modified to include patient advocates and the posting of information on the Internet detailing protocols, progress, and outcomes of NIH-funded clinical trials.

The NIH is also interested in possible future applications of gene therapy and has sponsored a gene therapy policy conference to discuss the use of this procedure for cosmetic enhancement, such as treatments for baldness. While favoring some cosmetic applications, RAC has made clear that it will not accept proposals for germ-line gene transfer experiments. The role of the RAC has evolved over the years from a regulatory body to an agency that provides a much-needed public forum that deals with the legal and ethical issues raised by gene therapy.

The Gelsinger Legal Trial

Jesse Gelsinger's death marked a crucial turning point in the regulation of gene therapy trials and in the public's attitude toward clinical trials in general. Initially, Jessie's father, Paul Gelsinger, trusted the medical staff involved in the trial that took his son's life, but as the FDA investigation progressed, it became clear to him that he had been naive. Consequently, in 2000 Paul Gelsinger and his brother John launched a civil lawsuit, in which the defendants were the trustees of the University of Pennsylvania, Dr. James Wilson and the company he cofounded, Genovo, Inc., and the attending physicians, Dr. Steven Raper and Dr. Mark Batshaw. Arthur Caplan, a bioethicist at the University of Pennsylvania, was also included for advice he gave to the other defendants. The lawsuit consisted of eight counts:

> *Count I—Wrongful Death* The plaintiffs in the case, Paul and John Gelsinger, charged that "as a result of the careless, negligent and

reckless conduct of the defendants herein, Jesse Gelsinger was caused to suffer excruciating and agonizing pain and discomfort and ultimately died as a result of defendants' conduct." The count further charges that the defendants failed to evaluate Jesse Gelsinger properly for admission into the trial, and that once admitted, failed to care for his condition under all of the circumstances, and by so doing failed to follow and abide by guidelines set forth by the FDA and NIH.

Count II—Survival Action   In causing Jesse Gelsinger's death, the defendants wrongfully deprived him of earnings and the right to earn a living. Consequently, the plaintiffs, acting on behalf of the Estate of Jesse Gelsinger, are entitled to recover an amount equal to the gross amount that Jesse would have earned from the date of his death to the end of his normal life expectancy.

Count III—Strict Products Liability   James Wilson and Genovo, Inc., manufactured and supplied the AD virus that ultimately caused the death of Jesse Gelsinger. The Institute of Human Gene Therapy (IHGT), as part of the University of Pennsylvania, is equally liable for supplying the same virus as part of the gene therapy trial. The defendants were further charged with designing, manufacturing, and selling a product that was poorly tested, defective, and dangerous. Moreover, the AD virus was sold without proper warnings on the product, and without warning the clinical subjects of the dangers inherent in using the product.

Count IV—Intentional Assault and Battery, Lack of Informed Consent   The defendants failed to warn Jesse Gelsinger of all of the risks involved in the therapy, without which he could not have been expected to give informed consent. The lack of informed consent involved several points that included, among others, understating the expected toxic effects of the virus, failing to describe the adverse effects experienced by previous patients in the trial, and the death of a monkey that received the virus in preclinical trials. The defendants also failed to disclose the financial interest that Dr. Wilson and the University of Pennsylvania had in relation to the study.

Count V—Intentional and Negligent Infliction of Emotional Distress   Paul Gelsinger's agreement to allow his son to take part in the study was based on the misleading information he was given by the defendants. As a consequence, he has suffered severe emotional distress for which he deserves compensation.

Count VI—Common Law Fraud/Intentional Misrepresentation The defendants committed fraud by intentionally misrepresenting the risks of the therapy and, in particular, the toxic side effects associated with the injection of the AD virus.

Count VII—Punitive Damages The plaintiffs maintained that the behavior of the defendants toward Jesse Gelsinger was "intentional, wanton, willful and outrageous. Defendants were grossly negligent, and acted with reckless disregard of and with deliberate, callous and reckless indifference to the rights, interests, welfare and safety of plaintiff's decedent."

Count VIII—Fraud on the FDA Defendants Batshaw, Raper, Wilson, IHGT, and Genovo "intentionally and falsely made numerous fraudulent misrepresentations to the FDA concerning the protocol of the OTC gene transfer experiment." It was also charged that the defendants altered the FDA approved consent form, deleting any reference to monkeys that became ill and died after receiving a similar AD vector in preclinical trials. Moreover, they defrauded the FDA by failing to report adverse and unexpected reactions associated with the administration of the vector.

Although committed to a jury trial in 2000, the University of Pennsylvania decided to settle out of court by paying the plaintiffs several million dollars in compensation. Paul Gelsinger has vowed to use the money to help improve patient safety in all clinical trials. Dr. Wilson resigned his position as director of IHGT in 2002, and the FDA is considering barring him from ever conducting further research on humans. Despite his resignation from IHGT, Dr. Wilson retains his faculty position and tenure at the University of Pennsylvania. Alan Milstein, the Gelsinger family's lawyer, had stated that the resignation is an inadequate consequence for Wilson's misdeeds that led to the death of Jesse Gelsinger. For its part, the university has never publicly apologized to the Gelsinger family, and according to Jesse's father, until that is done, the issue will never be fully resolved.

International Regulation

The United Kingdom and the European Union have formed gene therapy regulatory agencies that are very similar in organization to those established in the United States. Discussions in Europe began in 1991–92 and led to the formation in 1993 of the Gene Therapy Advisory Committee (GTAC) in the United Kingdom, and the European Agency for the Evaluation of Medicinal Products (EMEA).

GTAC reviews gene therapy proposals and makes recommendations to the Department of Health as to their acceptability. Their decision is based on scientific merit and the potential benefits and risks. The committee also provides advice to British health ministers on developments in gene therapy. The primary concern of GTAC is whether the gene therapy proposal meets accepted ethical criteria for research on human subjects as laid out by the Belmont Report and the Nuremberg Code. GTAC approval must be obtained before somatic cell gene therapy is conducted on human subjects. In accord with NIH regulations, GTAC will not allow gene therapy trials involving the germ line. This committee takes the view that gene therapy is not really therapy at all, but a research procedure, and therefore that all such trials must take place under strict rules established by GTAC. In contrast to FDA and NIH regulations, GTAC believes that gene therapy should be limited to life-threatening diseases or disorders. The European regulatory agency, EMEA, is in full accord with GTAC policies.

.8.

RESOURCE CENTER

Eukaryote Cell Primer

Life on earth began 3.5 billion years ago in the form of single cells that appeared in the oceans. These cells evolved into ancestral prokaryotes and, about 2 billion years ago, gave rise to Archaea, bacteria, and eukaryotes, the three major divisions of life in the world. Eukaryotes, in turn, gave rise to plants, animals, protozoans, and fungi. Each of these groups represents a distinct phylogenetic kingdom. The Archaea and bacteria represent a fifth kingdom, known as the monera or prokaryotes. Archaea and bacteria are very similar anatomically, both lacking a true nucleus and internal organelles. A prokaryote genome is a single circular piece of naked DNA called a chromosome, containing fewer than 5,000 genes. Eukaryotes (meaning true nucleus) are much more complex, having many membrane-bounded organelles. These include a nucleus, nucleolus, endoplasmic reticulum (ER), Golgi complex, mitochondria, lysosomes, and peroxisomes.

The eukaryote nucleus, bounded by a double phospholipid membrane, contains a DNA (deoxyribonucleic acid) genome on two or more linear chromosomes, each of which may contain up to 10,000 genes. The nucleus also contains an assembly plant for ribosomal subunits called the nucleolus. The endoplasmic reticulum (ER) and the Golgi complex work together to glycosylate proteins and lipids (attach sugar molecules to the proteins and lipids producing glycoproteins and glycolipids), most of which are destined for the cell membrane to form a molecular "forest" known as the glycocalyx. The glycoproteins and glycolipids travel from the ER to the Golgi, and from the Golgi to the

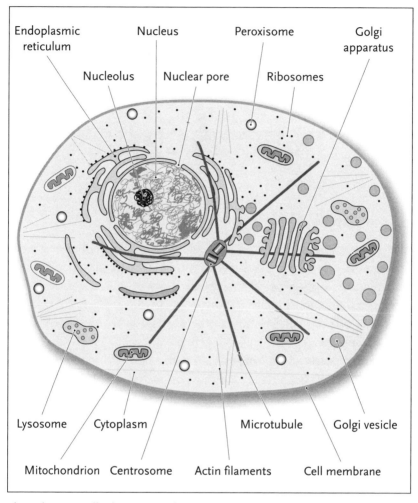

Endoplasmic reticulum · Nucleus · Peroxisome · Golgi apparatus

Nucleolus · Nuclear pore · Ribosomes

Lysosome · Cytoplasm · Microtubule · Golgi vesicle

Mitochondrion · Centrosome · Actin filaments · Cell membrane

The eukaryote cell. The structural components shown here are present in organisms as diverse as protozoans, plants, and animals. The nucleus contains the DNA genome and an assembly plant for ribosomal subunits (the nucleolus). The endoplasmic reticulum (ER) and the Golgi work together to modify proteins, most of which are destined for the cell membrane. These proteins are sent to the membrane in Golgi vesicles. Mitochondria provide the cell with energy in the form of ATP. Ribosomes, some of which are attached to the ER, synthesize proteins. Lysosomes and peroxisomes recycle cellular material and molecules. The microtubules and centrosome form the spindle apparatus for moving chromosomes to the daughter cells during cell division. Actin filaments and a weblike structure consisting of intermediate filaments (not shown) form the cytoskeleton.

cell surface, in membrane-bounded vesicles that form by budding off the organelle by exocytosis. Thus, the cytoplasm contains many transport vesicles that originate from the ER and Golgi. The Golgi vesicles bud off the outer chamber, or the one farthest from the ER. Mitochondria, once free-living prokaryotes, and the only other organelle with a double membrane, provide the cell with energy in the form of adenosine triphosphate (ATP). The production of ATP is carried out by an assembly of metal-containing proteins called the electron transport chain, located in the mitochondrion inner membrane. Ribosomes, some of which are attached to the ER, synthesize proteins. Lysosomes and peroxisomes recycle cellular material and molecules. The microtubules and centrosome form the spindle apparatus for moving chromosomes to the daughter cells during cell division. Actin filaments, and a weblike structure consisting of intermediate filaments form the cytoskeleton.

MOLECULES OF THE CELL

Cells are biochemical entities that synthesize many thousands of molecules. Studying these chemicals and the biochemistry of the cell would be a daunting task were it not for the fact that most of the chemical variation is based on six types of molecules which are assembled into just four types of macromolecules. The six basic molecules are amino acids, phosphate, glycerol, sugars, fatty acids, and nucleotides. Amino acids have a simple core structure consisting of an amino group, a carboxyl group, and a variable R group attached to a carbon atom. There are 20 different kinds of amino acids, each with a unique R group. Phosphates are extremely important molecules that are used in the construction or modification of many other molecules. They are also used to store chemical-bond energy. Glycerol is a simple three-carbon alcohol that is an important component of cell membranes and fat reservoirs. Sugars are extremely versatile molecules that are used as an energy source and for structural purposes. Glucose, a six-carbon sugar, is the primary energy source for most cells and it is the principal sugar used to glycosylate proteins and lipids for the production of the glycocalyx. Plants have exploited the structural potential of sugars in their production of cellulose and, thus, wood, bark, grasses, and reeds are polymers of glucose and other monosaccharides. Ribose, a five-carbon

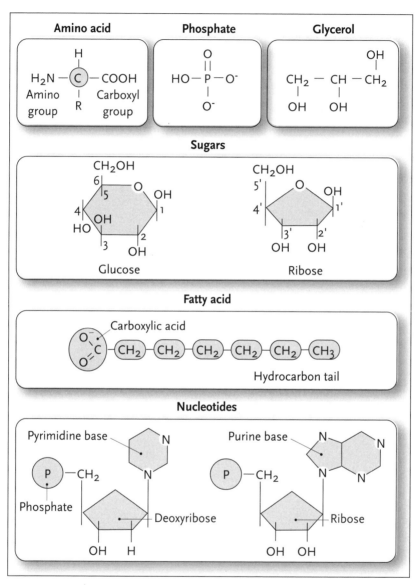

Molecules of the cell. Amino acids are the building blocks for proteins. Phosphate is an important component of many other molecules, and is added to proteins to modify their behavior. Glycerol is a three-carbon alcohol that is an important ingredient in cell membranes and fat. Sugars like glucose are a primary energy source for most cells, and also have many structural functions. Fatty acids are involved in the production of cell membranes and storage of fat. Nucleotides are the building blocks for DNA and RNA.

sugar, is a component of nucleic acids, as well as ATP. Ribose carbons are numbered as 1' (1 prime), 2' and so on. Consequently, references to nucleic acids, which include ribose, often refer to the 3' or 5' carbon. Fatty acids consist of a carboxyl group (when ionized it becomes a carboxylic acid) linked to a hydrophobic hydrocarbon tail. These molecules are used in the construction of cell membranes and fat.

Nucleotides are building blocks for DNA and RNA (ribonucleic acid). Nucleotides consist of three components: a phosphate, a ribose sugar, and a nitrogenous (nitrogen containing) ring compound that behaves as a base in solution. Nucleotide bases appear in two forms: A single-ring nitrogenous base called a pyrimidine, and a double-ringed base called a purine. There are two kinds of purines (adenine and guanine), and three pyrimidines (uracil, cytosine, and thymine). Uracil is specific to RNA, substituting for thymine. In addition, RNA nucleotides contain ribose, whereas DNA nucleotides contain deoxyribose (hence their names). Ribose has a hydroxyl (OH) group attached to both the 2' and 3' carbons, whereas deoxyribose is missing the 2' hydroxyl group. ATP, the molecule that is used by all cells as a source of energy, is a ribose nucleotide consisting of the purine base adenine and three phosphates attached to the 5' carbon of the ribose sugar. The phosphates are labeled α (alpha), β (beta) and γ (gamma), and are linked to the carbon in a tandem order, beginning with α. The energy stored by this molecule is carried by the covalent bonds of the β and γ phosphates. Breaking these bonds sequentially releases the energy they contain, while converting ATP to adenosine diphosphate (ADP) and then to adenosine monophosphate (AMP). AMP is converted back to ATP by mitochondria.

MACROMOLECULES OF THE CELL

The six basic molecules are used by all cells to construct five essential macromolecules. These include proteins, RNA, DNA, phospholipids, and sugar polymers, known as polysaccharides. Amino acids are linked together by peptide bonds to construct a protein. A peptide bond is formed by linking the carboxyl end of one amino acid to the amino end of second amino acid. Thus, once constructed, every protein has an amino end and a carboxyl end. An average protein may consist of 300–400 amino acids. Nucleic acids are macromolecules

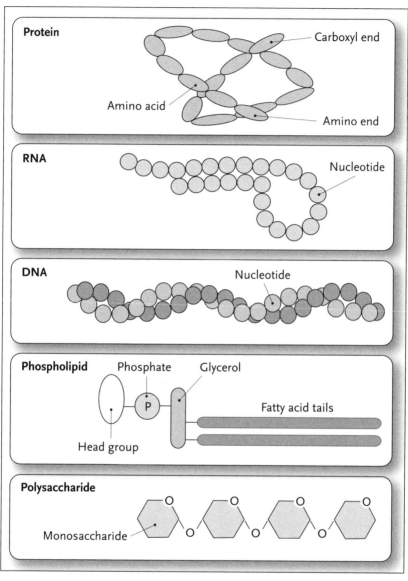

Macromolecules of the cell. Protein is made from amino acids linked together to form a long chain that can fold up into a three-dimensional structure. RNA and DNA are long chains of nucleotides. RNA is generally single stranded, but can form localized double-stranded regions. DNA is a double-stranded helix, with one strand coiling around the other. A phospholipid is composed of a hydrophilic head-group, a phosphate, a glycerol molecule, and two hydrophobic fatty-acid tails. Polysaccharides are sugar polymers.

constructed from nucleotides. The 5' phosphate of one nucleotide is linked to the 3' OH of a second nucleotide. Additional nucleotides are always linked to the 3' OH of the last nucleotide in the chain. Consequently, the growth of the chain is said to be in the 5' to 3' direction. RNA nucleotides are adenine, uracil, cytosine, and guanine. A typical RNA molecule consists of 2,000 to 3,000 nucleotides; it is generally single stranded, but can form localized double-stranded regions. RNA is involved in the synthesis of proteins and is a structural and enzymatic component of ribosomes. DNA, a double-stranded nucleic acid, encodes cellular genes and is constructed from adenine, thymine, cytosine, and guanine deoxyribonucleotides

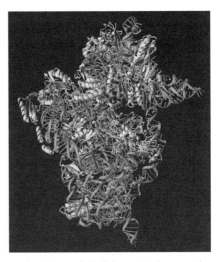

Molecule model of the 30S ribosomal subunit, which consists of protein (light gray corkscrew structures) and RNA (coiled ladders). The RNA that is also responsible for the catalytic function of the ribosome determines the overall shape of the molecule. *(Courtesy of V. Ramakrishnan, MRC Laboratory of Molecular Biology, Cambridge).*

(dATP, dTTP, dCTP and dGTP, where "d" indicates deoxyribose). The two DNA strands coil around each other like strands in a piece of rope, and for this reason the molecule is known as the double helix. DNA is an extremely large macromolecule, typically consisting of more than 1 million nucleotide pairs (or base pairs). Double-stranded DNA forms when two chains of nucleotides interact through the formation of chemical bonds between complementary base pairs. The chemistry of the bases is such that adenine pairs with thymine and cytosine pairs with guanine. For stability, the two strands are antiparallel, that is, the orientation of one strand is in the 5' to 3' direction, while the complementary strand runs 3' to 5'. Phospholipids, the main component of cell membranes, are composed of a polar head group (usually an alcohol), a phosphate, glycerol, and two hydrophobic fatty-acid tails. Fat that is

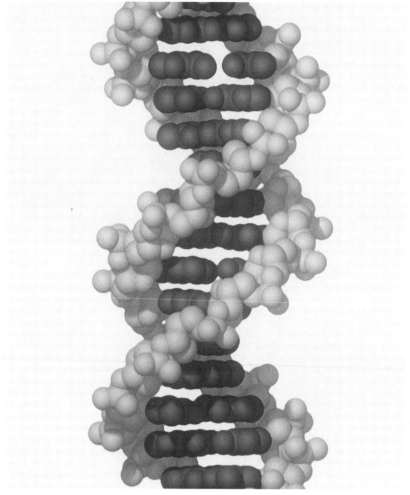

Computer model of DNA. The two strands coil around each other to form a helix that, when looking down on it from above, coils to the right. The spherical structures in this image represent the various atoms in the sugars and bases (dark gray), and phosphates (light gray). *(Kenneth Eward/ BioGrafx/Photo Researchers, Inc.)*

stored in the body as an energy reserve has a structure similar to a phospholipid, being composed of three fatty acid chains attached to a molecule of glycerol. The third fatty acid takes the place of the phosphate and head group of a phospholipid. Sugars are polymerized to form chains of two or more monosaccharides. Disaccharides (two monosaccharides) and oligosaccharides (three to 12 monosaccharides) are attached to proteins and lipids destined for the glycocalyx. Polysaccharides, such as glycogen and starch, may contain several hundred monosaccharides and are stored in cells as an energy reserve.

THE CELL CYCLE

Cells inherited the power of reproduction from prebiotic bubbles that split in half at regular intervals under the influence of the turbulent environment that characterized the Earth more than 3 billion years ago. This pattern of turbulent fragmentation followed by a brief period of calm is now a regular behavior pattern of every cell. Even today, after 3 billion years, many cells still divide every 20 minutes.

The regular alternation between division and calm has come to be known as the cell cycle. In studying this cycle, scientists have recognized different states of calm and different ways in which a cell can divide. The calm state of the cell cycle, referred to as interphase, is divided into three sub-phases called Gap 1 (G_1), S phase (a period of DNA synthesis) and Gap 2 (G_2). The conclusion of interphase, and with it the termination of G_2, occurs with division of the cell and a return to G_1. Cells may leave the cycle by entering a special phase called G_0. Some cells, such as postmitotic neurons in an animal's brain, remain in G_0 for the life of the organism.

Although interphase is a period of relative calm, the cell

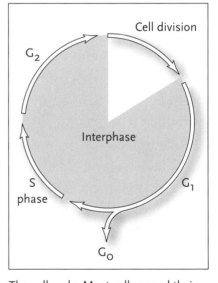

The cell cycle. Most cells spend their time cycling between a state of calm (interphase) and cell division. Interphase is further divided into three subphases: Gap 1 (G_1), S phase (DNA synthesis), and Gap 2 (G_2). Cells may exit the cycle by entering a special phase called G_0.

grows continuously during this period, working hard to prepare for the next round of division. Two notable events are the duplication of the spindle (the centrosome and associated microtubules), a structure that is crucial for the movement of the chromosomes during cell division, and the appearance of an enzyme called maturation promoting factor (MPF) at the end of G_2. MPF phosphorylates histones. Histones are proteins that bind to the DNA, which when phosphorylated, compacts (or condenses) the chromosomes in preparation for cell division. MPF is also responsible for the breakdown of the nuclear membrane. When cell division is complete, MPF disappears, allowing the chromosomes to decondense and the nuclear envelope to re-form. Completion of a normal cell cycle always involves the division of a cell into two daughter cells. This can occur by a process known as mitosis, which is intended for cell multiplication, and by a second process known as meiosis, which is intended for sexual reproduction.

MITOSIS

Mitosis is used by all free-living eukaryotes (protozoans) as a means of asexual reproduction. The growth of a plant or an animal is also accomplished with this form of cell division. Mitosis is divided into four stages: prophase, metaphase, anaphase, and telophase. All of these stages are marked out in accordance with the behavior of the nucleus and the chromosomes. Prophase marks the period during which the duplicated chromosomes begin condensation and the two centrosomes begin moving to opposite poles of the cell. Under the microscope, the chromosomes become visible as X-shaped structures, which are the two duplicated chromosomes, often called sister chromatids. A special region of each chromosome, called a centromere, holds the chromatids together. Proteins bind to the centromere to form a structure called the kinetochore (see the figure on page 97). Metaphase is a period during which the chromosomes are sorted out and aligned between the two centrosomes. By this time, the nuclear membrane has completely broken down. The two centrosomes and the microtubules fanning out between them form the mitotic spindle. The area in between the spindles, where the chromosomes are aligned, is often referred to as the metaphase plate. Some of the microtubules make contact with the kinetochores, while others overlap, with motor proteins situated in between. Eukaryotes are

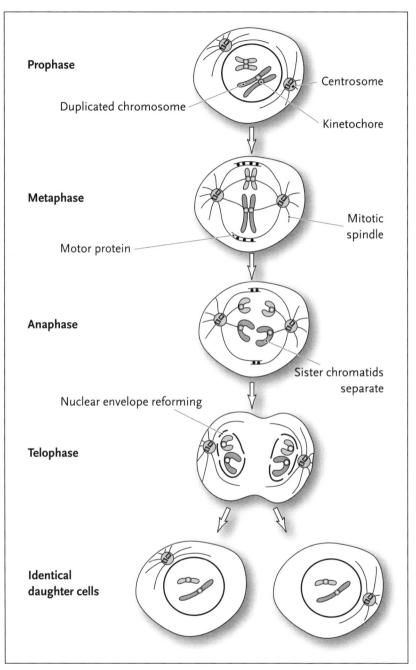

Prophase

Duplicated chromosome

Centrosome

Kinetochore

Metaphase

Motor protein

Mitotic spindle

Anaphase

Sister chromatids separate

Nuclear envelope reforming

Telophase

Identical daughter cells

Mitosis. Principal stages deal with the movement and partitioning of the chromosomes between the future daughter cells. For clarity, only two chromosomes are shown.

normally diploid, so a cell would have two copies of each chromosome, one from the mother and one from the father. Anaphase is characterized by the movement of the duplicated chromosomes to opposite poles of the cell. The first step is the release of an enzyme that breaks the bonds holding the kinetochores together, thus allowing the sister chromatids to separate from each other while remaining bound to their respective microtubules. Motor proteins then move along the microtubule, dragging the chromosomes to opposite ends of the cell. Using energy supplied by ATP, the motor proteins break the microtubule down as it drags the chromosome along, so that the microtubule is gone by the time the chromosome reaches the spindle pole. Throughout this process, the motor proteins and the chromosome manage to stay one step ahead of the disintegrating microtubule. The overlapping microtubules aid movement of the chromosomes toward the poles as another type of motor protein pushes the microtubules in opposite directions, effectively forcing the centrosomes toward the poles. This accounts for the greater overlap of microtubules in metaphase as compared with anaphase. During telophase, the daughter chromosomes arrive at the spindle poles and decondense to form the relaxed chromatin characteristic of interphase nuclei. The nuclear envelope begins forming around the chromosomes, marking the end of mitosis. During the same period, a contractile ring, made of the proteins myosin and actin, begins pinching the parental cell in two. This stage, separate from mitosis, is called cytokinesis, and leads to the formation of two daughter cells, each with one nucleus.

MEIOSIS

Unlike mitosis, which leads to the growth of an organism, meiosis is intended for sexual reproduction and occurs exclusively in ovaries and testes. Eukaryotes, being diploid, receive chromosomes from both parents; if gametes were produced using mitosis, a catastrophic growth in the number of chromosomes would occur each time a sperm fertilized an egg. Meiosis is a special form of cell division that produces haploid gametes (eggs and sperm), each possessing half as many chromosomes as the diploid cell. When haploid gametes fuse, they produce an embryo with the correct number of chromosomes.

The existence of meiosis was first suggested 100 years ago when microbiologists counted the number chromosomes in somatic and

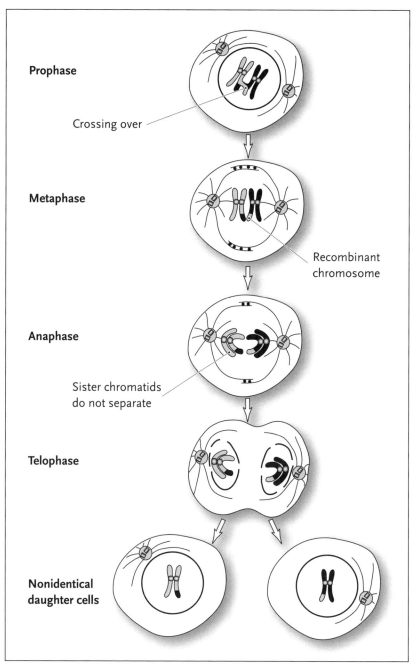

Prophase

Crossing over

Metaphase

Recombinant chromosome

Anaphase

Sister chromatids do not separate

Telophase

Nonidentical daughter cells

Meiosis I. The most notable features include genetic recombination (crossing over) between the homologous chromosomes during prophase, comigration of the sister chromatids during anaphase, and the production of nonidentical daughter cells. Only one homologous pair is shown.

germ cells. The roundworm, for example, was found to have four chromosomes in its somatic cells but only two in its gametes. Many other studies also compared the amount of DNA in nuclei from somatic cells and gonads, always with the same result: The amount of DNA in somatic cells is exactly double the amount in fully mature gametes. To understand how this could be, scientists studied cell division in the gonads and were able to show that meiosis occurs as two rounds of cell division with only one round of DNA synthesis. The two rounds of division were called meiosis I and meiosis II, and scientists observed that both could be divided into the same four stages known to occur in mitosis. Indeed, meiosis II is virtually identical to a mitotic division. Meiosis I resembles mitosis, but close examination shows three important differences: gene swapping occurs between homologous chromosomes in prophase; homologs (that is, two homologous chromosomes) remain paired at metaphase, instead of lining up at the plate as is done in mitosis; and the kinetochores do not separate at anaphase.

Homologous chromosomes are two identical chromosomes that come from different parents. For example, humans have 23 chromosomes from the father and the same 23 from the mother. We each have a maternal chromosome 1 and a paternal chromosome 1; they carry the same genes but specify slightly different traits. Chromosome 1 may carry the gene for eye color, but the maternal version, or allele, may specify blue eyes, whereas the paternal allele specifies brown. During prophase, homologous pairs exchange large numbers of genes by swapping whole pieces of chromosome. Thus one of the maternal chromatids (gray in the figure on page 99) ends up with a piece of paternal chromosome, and a paternal chromatid receives the corresponding piece of maternal chromosome. Mixing genetic material in this way is unique to meiosis, and it is one of the reasons sexual reproduction has been such a powerful evolutionary force.

During anaphase of meiosis I, the kinetochores do not separate as they do in mitosis. The effect of this is to separate the maternal and paternal chromosomes by sending them to different daughter cells, although the segregation is random. That is, the daughter cells receive a random assortment of maternal and paternal chromosomes, rather than one daughter cell receiving all paternal chromosomes and the other all maternal chromosomes. Random segregation, along with genetic recombination, accounts for the fact that while children resemble their parents, they do not look or act exactly like them. These two mechanisms are responsible for the remarkable adaptability of all eukaryotes. Meiosis II begins immediately after the completion of meiosis I, which produces two daughter cells, each containing a duplicated parent chromosome and a recombinant chromosome consisting of both paternal and maternal DNA. These two cells divide mitotically to produce four haploid cells, each of which is genetically unique, containing unaltered or recombinant maternal and paternal chromosomes. Meiosis produces haploid cells by passing through two rounds of cell division with only one round of DNA synthesis. However, as we have seen, the process is not just concerned with reducing the number of chromosomes but is also involved in stirring up the genetic pot in order to produce unique gametes that may someday give rise to an equally unique individual.

DNA REPLICATION

DNA replication, which occurs during the S phase of the cell cycle, requires the coordinated effort of a team of enzymes, led by DNA helicase and primase. The helicase is a remarkable enzyme that is responsible for separating the two DNA strands, a feat that it accomplishes at an astonishing rate of 1,000 nucleotides every second. This enzyme gets its name from the fact that it unwinds the DNA helix as it separates the two strands. The enzyme that is responsible for reading the template strand and for synthesizing the new daughter strand is called DNA polymerase. This enzyme reads the parental DNA in the 3' to 5' direction and creates a daughter strand that grows 5' to 3'. DNA polymerase also has an editorial function, in that it checks the preceding nucleotide to make sure it is correct before it adds a nucleotide to the growing chain. The editor function of this enzyme introduces an interesting problem. How can the polymerase add the very first nucleotide when it has to check a preceding nucleotide before adding a new one? A special enzyme called primase, which is attached to the helicase, solves this problem. Primase synthesizes short pieces of RNA that form a DNA-RNA double-stranded region. The RNA becomes a temporary part of the daughter strand, thus priming the DNA polymerase by providing the crucial first nucleotide in the new strand. Once the chromosome is

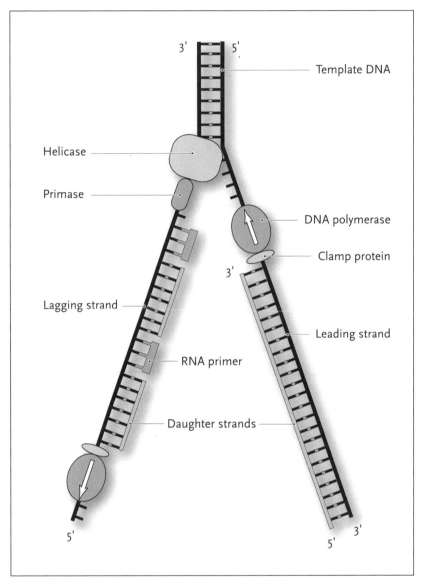

DNA replication. The helicase separates the two strands so the DNA polymerase can synthesize new strands. The primase provides replication signals for the polymerase in the form of RNA primers, and the clamp protein keeps the polymerase from falling off the DNA. The leading strand requires only a single primer (not shown). The lagging strand requires many primers, and the daughter strand is synthesized as a series of DNA fragments that are later joined into one continuous strand.

duplicated, DNA repair enzymes remove the RNA primers and replace them with DNA nucleotides.

TRANSCRIPTION, TRANSLATION, AND THE GENETIC CODE

Genes encode proteins and several kinds of RNA. Extracting the information from DNA requires the processes of transcription and translation. Transcription, catalyzed by the enzyme RNA polymerase, copies one strand of the DNA into a complementary strand of messenger RNA (mRNA) or ribosomal RNA (rRNA) that is used in the construction of ribosomes. Messenger RNA translocates to the cytoplasm where it is translated into a protein by ribosomes. Newly transcribed rRNA is sent to the nucleolus for ribosome assembly, and is never translated. Ribosomes are complex structures consisting of about 50 proteins and four kinds of rRNA, known as 5S, 5.8S, 18S, and 28S rRNA (the "S" refers to a sedimentation coefficient that is proportional to size). These RNAs range in size from about 500 bases up to the 2,000 bases of the 28S. The ribosome is assembled in the nucleolus as two nonfunctional subunits before being sent out to the cytoplasm where the subunits combine, along with an mRNA, to form a fully functional unit. The production of ribosomes in this way ensures that translation never occurs in the nucleus.

The genetic code provides a way for the translation machinery to interpret the sequence information stored in the DNA molecule and represented by mRNA. DNA is a linear sequence of four different kinds of nucleotides, so the simplest code could be one in which each nucleotide specifies a different amino acid—that is, adenine coding for the amino acid glycine, cytosine for lysine, and so on. The first cells may have used this coding system, but it is limited to the construction of proteins consisting of only four different kinds of amino acids. Eventually, a more elaborate code evolved, in which a combination of three out of the four possible DNA nucleotides, called codons, specifies a single amino acid. With this scheme it is possible to have a unique code for each of the 20 naturally occurring amino acids. For example, the codon AGC specifies the amino acid serine, whereas TGC specifies the amino acid cysteine. Thus, a gene may be viewed as a long continuous sequence of codons. However, not all codons specify an amino acid. The

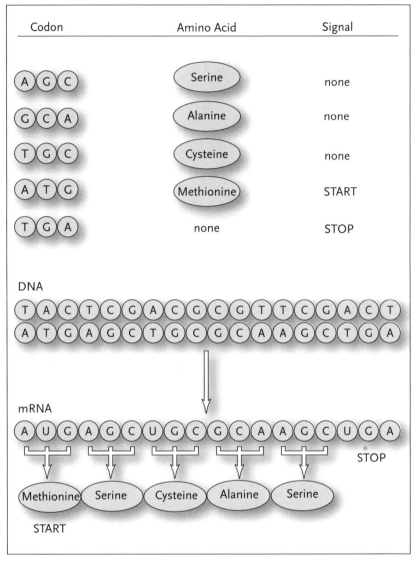

Transcription, translation, and the genetic code. Five codons are shown, four specifying amino acids (protein subunits), and two of the five serving as start and stop signals. The codons, including the start and stop signals, are linked together to form a gene on the bottom, or coding, DNA strand. The coding strand is copied into messenger RNA (mRNA), which is used to synthesize the protein. Nucleotides appear as round beads: adenine (A), thymine (T), cytosine (C) and guanine (G). Amino acids appear as labeled elliptical beads. Note that in mRNA uracil (U) replaces the thymine (T) found in DNA.

sequence TGA signals the end of the gene, and a special codon, ATG, signals the start site, in addition to specifying the amino acid methionine. Consequently, all proteins begin with this amino acid, although it is sometimes removed once construction of the protein is complete. As mentioned above, an average protein may consist of 300 to 400 amino acids; since the codon consists of three nucleotides for each amino acid, a typical gene may be 900 to 1,200 nucleotides long.

POWER GENERATION

ATP is produced in mitochondria from AMP or ADP and phosphate (PO_4). This process involves a number of metal-binding proteins called the respiratory chain (also known as the electron transport chain), and a special ion channel–enzyme called ATP synthetase. The respiratory chain consists of three major components: NADH dehydrogenase, cytochrome b, and cytochrome oxidase. All of these components are protein complexes that have an iron (NADH dehydrogenase, cytochrome b) or a copper core (cytochrome oxidase) and, together with the ATP synthetase, are located in the inner membrane of the mitochondria.

The respiratory chain is analogous to an electric cable that transports electricity from a hydroelectric dam to our homes, where it is used to turn on lights or to power our stereos. The human body, like that of all animals, generates electricity by processing food molecules through a metabolic pathway called the Krebs cycle. The electricity, or electrons so generated, travel through the respiratory chain, and as they do, they power the synthesis of ATP. All electrical circuits must have a ground, that is, the electrons need some place to go once they have completed the circuit. In the case of the respiratory chain, the ground is oxygen. After passing through the chain, the electrons are picked up by oxygen, which combines with hydrogen ions to form water.

THE GLYCOCALYX

This structure is an enormously diverse collection of glycoproteins and glycolipids that covers the surface of every cell, like trees on the surface of the Earth, and has many important functions. All eukaryotes originated from free-living cells that hunted bacteria for food. The glycocalyx evolved to meet the demands of this kind of lifestyle, providing a way for the cell to locate, capture, and ingest food molecules or prey organisms. Cell-surface glycoproteins also form transporters and ion channels that serve as gateways into the cell. Neurons have refined ion

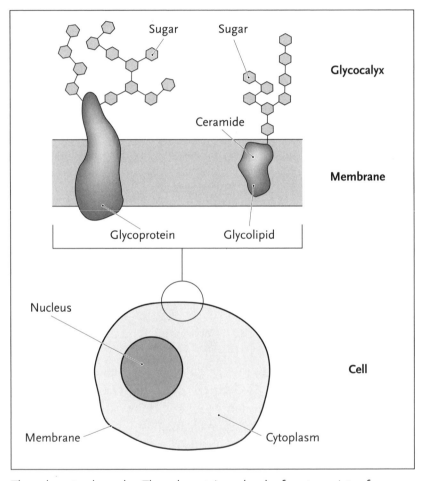

The eukaryote glycocalyx. The eukaryote's molecular forest consists of glycoproteins and glycolipids. Two examples are shown at the top, a glycoprotein on the left, and a glycolipid on the right. The glycoprotein trees have "trunks" made of protein and "leaves" made of sugar molecules. Glycolipids also have "leaves" made of sugar molecules, but the "trunks" are a fatty compound called ceramide that is completely submerged within the plane of the membrane. The glycocalyx has many jobs, including cell-to-cell communication and the transport and detection of food molecules. It also provides recognition markers so the immune system can detect foreign cells.

channels for the purpose of cell-to-cell communication, giving rise to the nervous systems found in most animal species. In higher vertebrates, certain members of the glycocalyx are used by cells of the immune system as recognition markers to detect invading microbes or foreign cells introduced as an organ or tissue transplant.

Recombinant DNA Primer

Recombinant technology is a collection of procedures that make it possible to isolate a gene and produce enough of it for a detailed study of its structure and function. Central to this technology is the ability to construct libraries of DNA fragments that represent the genetic repertoire of an entire organism or of a specific cell type. Constructing these libraries involves splicing different pieces of DNA together to form a novel or recombinant genetic entity, from which the procedure derives its name. DNA cloning and Library construction were made possible by the discovery of DNA-modifying enzymes that can seal two pieces of DNA together or can cut DNA at sequence-specific sites. Many of the procedures that are part of recombinant technology, such as DNA sequencing or filter hybridization, were developed to characterize DNA fragments that were isolated from cells or gene libraries. Obtaining the sequence of a gene has made it possible to study the organization of the genome, but more important, it has provided a simple way of determining the protein sequence and the expression profile for any gene.

DNA-MODIFYING ENZYMES

Two of the most important enzymes used in recombinant technology are those that can modify DNA by sealing two fragments together and others that can cut DNA at specific sites. The first modifying enzyme to be discovered was DNA ligase, an enzyme that can join two pieces of DNA together. It is an important component of the cell's DNA replication and repair machinery. Other DNA modifying enzymes, called restriction enzymes, cut DNA at sequence-specific sites, with different members of the family cutting at different sites. Restriction enzymes are isolated from bacteria, and since their discovery in 1970, more than 90 such enzymes have been isolated from more than 230 bacterial strains.

The name "restriction enzyme" is cryptic, and calls for an explanation. During the period when prokaryotes began to appear on Earth, their environment contained a wide assortment of molecules that were released into the soil or water by other cells, either deliberately or when the cells died. DNA of varying lengths was among these molecules, and was readily taken up by living cells. If the foreign DNA contained complete genes from a competing bacterial species, there was the real possibility that those genes could have been transcribed and translated by the host cell with potentially fatal results. As a precaution, prokaryotes evolved a set of enzymes that would restrict the foreign DNA population by cutting it up into smaller pieces, before being broken down completely to individual nucleotides.

GEL ELECTROPHORESIS

This procedure is used to separate different DNA and RNA fragments in a slab of agar or polyacrylamide subjected to an electric field. Nucleic acids carry a negative charge and thus will migrate toward a positively charged electrode. The gel acts a sieving medium that impedes the movement of the molecules. Thus, the rate at which the fragments migrate is a function of their size; small fragments migrate more rapidly than large fragments. The gel, containing the samples, is submerged in a special pH-regulated solution, or buffer, containing a nucleic acid–specific dye, ethidium bromide. This dye produces a strong reddish-yellow fluorescence when exposed to ultraviolet (UV) radiation. Consequently, after electrophoresis, the nucleic acid can be detected by photographing the gel under UV illumination.

DNA CLONING

In 1973 scientists discovered that restriction enzymes, DNA ligase, and bacterial plasmids could be used to clone DNA molecules. Plasmids are small (about 4,000 base pairs, also expressed as 4.0 kilo base pairs or 4 Kbp) circular minichromosomes that occur naturally in bacteria and are often exchanged between cells by passive diffusion. When a bacterium acquires a new plasmid it is said to have been transfected. For bacteria, the main advantage to swapping plasmids is that they often carry antibiotic resistance genes, so that a cell sensitive to ampicillin can become resistant simply by acquiring the right plasmid.

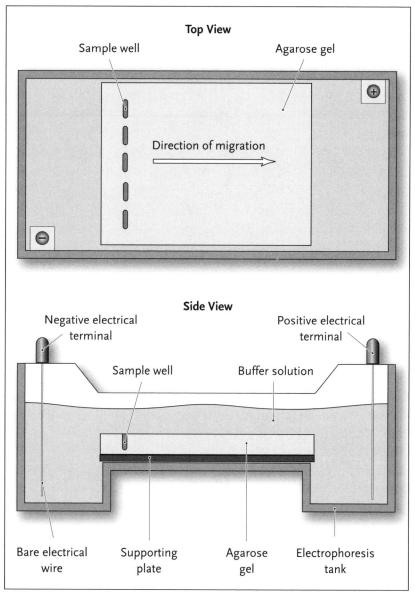

Top View

Sample well

Agarose gel

Direction of migration

Side View

Negative electrical terminal

Positive electrical terminal

Sample well

Buffer solution

Bare electrical wire

Supporting plate

Agarose gel

Electrophoresis tank

Agarose gel electrophoresis. An agarose gel is placed in an electrophoresis tank and submerged in a buffer solution. The electrical terminals are connected to a power source, with the sample wells positioned near the negative terminal. When the current is turned on, the negatively charged nucleic acids migrate towards the positive terminal. The migration rate is an inverse function of molecular size. (Large molecules travel more slowly than small ones.)

The first cloning experiment used a plasmid from *Escherichia coli* that was cut with the restriction enzyme *Eco*RI. The plasmid had a single *Eco*RI site, so the restriction enzyme simply opened the circular

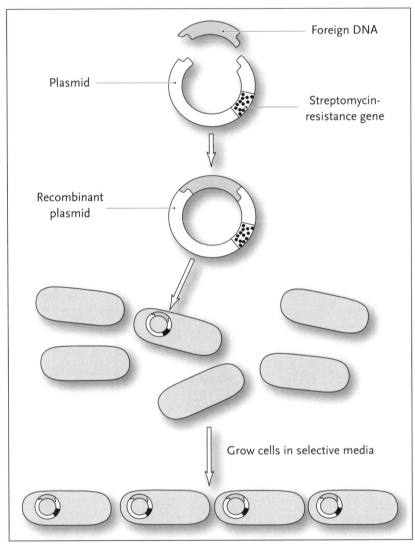

Cloning DNA in a plasmid. The foreign DNA and the plasmid are cut with the same restriction enzyme, allowed to fuse, and then sealed with DNA ligase. The recombinant plasmid is mixed with bacterial cells, some of which pick up the plasmid, allowing them to grow in a culture medium containing the antibiotic streptomycin. The bacteria's main chromosome is not shown.

molecule, rather than cutting it up into many useless pieces. Foreign DNA, cut with the same restriction enzyme, was incubated with the plasmid. Because the plasmid and foreign DNA were both cut with *Eco*RI, the DNA could insert itself into the plasmid to form a hybrid, or recombinant plasmid, after which DNA ligase sealed the two together. The reaction mixture was added to a small volume of *E. coli* so that some of the cells could take up the recombinant plasmid before being transferred to a nutrient broth containing streptomycin. Only those cells carrying the recombinant plasmid, which contained an antistreptomycin gene, could grow in the presence of this antibiotic. Each time the cells divided, the plasmid DNA was duplicated along with the main chromosome. After the cells had grown overnight, the foreign DNA had been amplified, or cloned, billions of times and was easily isolated for sequencing or expression studies.

GENOMIC AND cDNA LIBRARIES

The basic cloning procedure described above not only provides a way to amplify a specific piece of DNA, but it can also be used to construct gene libraries. In this case, however, the cloning vector is a bacteriophage, called lambda. The lambda genome is double-stranded linear DNA of about 40 Kbp, much of which can be replaced by foreign DNA without sacrificing the ability of the virus to infect bacteria. This is the great advantage of lambda over a plasmid. Lambda can accommodate very long pieces of DNA, often long enough to contain an entire gene, whereas a plasmid cannot accommodate foreign DNA that is larger than 4 Kbp. Moreover, bacteriophage has the natural ability to infect bacteria, so that the efficiency of transfection is 100 times greater than it is for plasmids.

The construction of a gene library begins by isolating genomic DNA and digesting it with a restriction enzyme to produce fragments of 1,000 to 10,000 base pairs. These fragments are ligated into lambda genomes, which are subjected to a packaging reaction to produce mature viral particles, most of which carry a different piece of the genomic DNA. This collection of viruses is called a genomic library and is used to study the structure and organization of specific genes. Clones from such a library contain the coding sequences, in addition to introns, intervening sequences, promoters, and enhancers. An alternative form of gene library can be constructed by isolating mRNA from a specific cell type. This RNA is converted to the complementary DNA (cDNA) using an RNA-dependent DNA polymerase called reverse transcriptase. The cDNA is ligated to lambda genomes and packaged as for the genomic library. This collection of recombinant viruses is a cDNA library and contains only genes that were being expressed by the cells when the RNA was extracted. It does not include introns or controlling elements as these are lost during transcription and the processing that occurs in the cell to make mature mRNA. Thus a cDNA library is intended for the purpose of studying gene expression and the structure of the coding region only.

LABELING CLONED DNA

Many of the procedures used in the area of recombinant technology were inspired by the events that occur during DNA replication. This includes the labeling of cloned DNA for use as probes in expression studies, DNA sequencing, and polymerase chain reaction (PCR, described in a following section). DNA replication involves duplicating one of the strands (the parent, or template strand) by linking nucleotides in an order specified by the template, and depends on a large number of enzymes, the most important of which is DNA polymerase. This enzyme, guided by the template strand, constructs a daughter strand by linking nucleotides together. One such nucleotide is deoxyadenine triphosphate (dATP). Deoxyribonucleotides have a single hydroxyl group located at the 3' carbon of the sugar group, while the triphosphate is attached to the 5' carbon. The procedure for labeling DNA probes, developed in 1983, introduces radioactive nucleotides into a DNA molecule. This method supplies DNA polymerase with a single-stranded DNA template, a primer, and the four nucleotides in a buffered solution to induce in vitro replication. The daughter strand that becomes the probe is labeled by including a nucleotide in the reaction mix that is linked to a radioactive isotope. The radioactive nucleotide is usually deoxycytosine triphosphate (dCTP) or dATP.

Single-stranded DNA hexamers (six bases long) are used as primers, and these are produced in such a way that they contain all possible permutations of four bases taken six at a time. Randomizing the base sequence for the primers ensures that there will be at least one primer site in a template that is only 50 bp long. Templates used in labeling reactions such as this are generally 100 to 800 bp long. This strategy of labeling DNA, known as random primer or oligo labeling, is widely used in cloning and in DNA and RNA filter hybridizations (described in following sections).

DNA SEQUENCING

A sequencing reaction developed by the British biochemist Dr. Fred Sanger in 1976 is another technique that takes its inspiration from the natural process of DNA replication. DNA polymerase requires a primer with a free 3' hydroxyl group. The polymerase adds the first nucleotide to this group, and all subsequent bases are added to the 3' hydroxyl of the previous base. Sequencing by the Sanger method is usually performed with the DNA cloned into a plasmid. This simplifies the choice of the initial primers since their sequence can be derived from the known plasmid sequence. An engineered plasmid primer site adjacent to a cloned DNA fragment is shown in the accompanying figure at right. Once the primer binds to the primer site the cloned DNA may be replicated. Sanger's innovation involved the synthesis of artificial nucleotides lacking the 3' hydroxyl group, thus producing dideoxynucleotides (ddATP, ddCTP, ddGTP and ddTTP). Incorporation of a dideoxynucleotide terminates the growth of the daughter strand at that point, and this can be used to

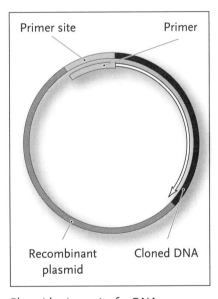

Plasmid primer site for DNA sequencing. The cloned DNA is inserted into the plasmid near an engineered primer site. Once the primer binds to the primer site, the cloned DNA may be replicated as part of a sequencing reaction in the direction indicated by the arrow. Only one strand of the double-stranded plasmid, and cloned DNA, is shown.

determine the size of each daughter strand. The shortest daughter strand represents the complementary nucleotide at the beginning of the template, whereas the longest strand represents the complementary nucleotide at the end of the template (see table below). The reaction products, consisting of all the daughter strands, are fractionated on a polyacrylamide gel. Polyacrylamide serves the same function as agarose. It has the advantage of being a tougher material, essential for the large size of a typical sequencing gel. Some of the nucleotides included in the Sanger reaction are labeled with a radioactive isotope so the fractionated daughter strands can be visualized by drying the gel and then exposing it to X-ray film. Thus, the Sanger method uses the natural process of replication to mark the position of each nucleotide in the DNA fragment so the sequence of the fragment can be determined.

A representation of a sequencing gel is shown in the figure on page 115. The sequence of the daughter strand is read beginning with

EXAMPLE OF A SEQUENCING REACTION	
Tube	**Reaction Products**
A	G-C-A-T-C-G-T-C G-C-A-T-C-G-T-C C-G-T-**A** C-G-T-A-G-C-**A**
T	G-C-A-T-C-G-T-C C-G-**T**
C	G-C-A-T-C-G-T-C G-C-A-T-C-G-T-C **C** C-G-T-A-G-**C**
G	G-C-A-T-C-G-T-C G-C-A-T-C-G-T-C C-**G** C-G-T-A-**G** G-C-A-T-C-G-T-C C-G-T-A-G-C-A-**G**

The Sanger sequencing reaction is set up in four separate tubes, each containing a different dideoxynucleotide (ddATP, ddTTP, ddCTP, and ddGTP). The reaction products are shown for each of the tubes: A (ddATP), T (ddTTP), C (ddCTP), and G (ddGTP). The template strand is GCATCGTC. Replication of the template begins after the primer binds to the primer site on the sequencing plasmid. The dideoxynucleotide terminating the reaction is shown in bold. The daughter strands, all of different lengths, are fractionated on a polyacrylamide gel.

the smallest fragment at the bottom of the gel, and ending with the largest fragment at the top. The sequence of the template strand (see table on page 114) is obtained simply by taking the complement of the sequence obtained from the gel (the daughter strand).

SOUTHERN AND NORTHERN BLOTTING

One of the most important techniques to be developed, as part of recombinant technology, is the transfer of nucleic acids from an agarose gel to nylon filter paper that can be hybridized to a labeled probe to detect specific genes. This procedure was introduced by the Scottish scientist E. M. Southern in 1975 for transferring DNA and is now known as Southern blotting. Since the DNA is transferred to filter paper, the detection stage is known as filter hybridization. In 1980 the procedure was modified to transfer RNA to nylon membranes for the study of gene expression and, in reference to the original, is called northern blotting.

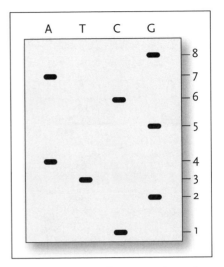

A representation of a sequencing gel. The reaction products (shown in the table on page 114) run from the top to the bottom, with the smallest fragment migrating at the highest rate. The sequence is read beginning with the smallest fragment on the gel (band 1, in the "C" lane) and ending with the largest fragment at the top (band 8, in the "G" lane). The sequence is CGTAGCAG. The complementary sequence is GCATCGTC. This is the template strand indicated in the table.

Northern blotting is used to study the expression of specific genes and is usually performed on messenger RNA (mRNA). Typical experiments may wish to determine the expression of specific genes in normal versus cancerous tissue, or in tissues obtained from groups of different ages. The RNA is fractionated on an agarose gel and then transferred to a nylon membrane. Paper towels placed on top of the assembly pull the transfer buffer through the gel, eluting the RNA from the gel and trapping it on the membrane. The location of specific mRNA can be determined by hybridizing the membrane to a radiolabeled cDNA or genomic clone.

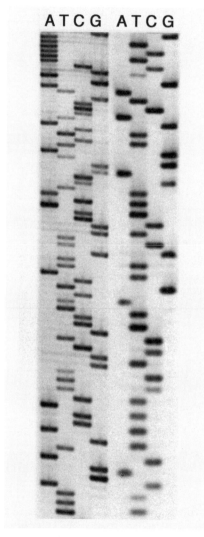

The hybridization procedure involves placing the filter in a buffer solution containing a labeled probe. During a long incubation period, the probe binds to the target sequence immobilized on the membrane. A-T and G-C base pairing mediate the binding between the probe and target. The double-stranded molecule that is formed is a hybrid, being formed between the RNA target, on the membrane, and the DNA probe.

FLUORESCENT IN SITU HYBRIDIZATION (FISH)

Studying gene expression does not always depend on northern blots and filter hybridization. In the 1980s scientists found that cDNA probes could be hybridized to DNA or mRNA in situ, that is, while located within cells or tissue sections fixed on microscope slides. In this case the probe is labeled with a fluorescent dye molecule, rather than a radioactive isotope. The samples are then examined and photographed under a fluorescent microscope. FISH is an extremely powerful variation on Southern and northern blots. This procedure gives precise

An autoradiogram of a portion of a DNA sequencing gel. A partial sequence (the first 20 bases) of the left set, beginning at the bottom of the "T" lane, is TTTAGGATGACCACTTTGGC. *(Dr. Joseph P. Panno)*

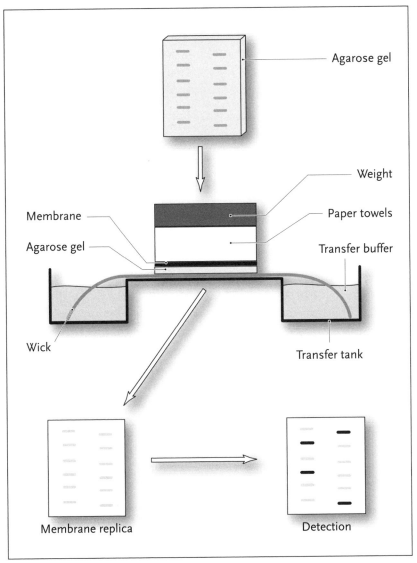

Northern transfer and membrane hybridization. RNA is fractionated on an agarose gel and then placed face down on a paper wick in a transfer tank. The gel is overlain with a piece of nylon membrane, paper towels, and weight. The paper towels draw the buffer through the gel and the membrane. The flow of buffer elutes the RNA from the gel, transferring it to the membrane. A radiolabeled cDNA probe is hybridized to the membrane to detect specific mRNA transcripts. Note that the thickness of the membrane is exaggerated for clarity.

information regarding the identity of a cell that expresses a specific gene, information that usually cannot be obtained with filter hybridization. Organs and tissues are generally composed of many different kinds of cells that cannot be separated from each other using standard biochemical extraction procedures. Histological sections, however, show clearly the various cell types, and when subjected to FISH analysis provide clear results as to which cells express specific genes. FISH is also used in clinical laboratories for the diagnosis of genetic abnormalities.

POLYMERASE CHAIN REACTION (PCR)

PCR is simply repetitive DNA replication over a limited, primer defined, region of a suitable template. The region defined by the primers is amplified to such an extent that it can be easily isolated for further study. The reaction exploits the fact that a DNA duplex, in a low-salt butter, will melt (that is, separate into two single strands) at 75°C, but will reanneal (rehybridize) at 37°C. The reaction is initiated by melting the template, in the presence of primers and polymerase in a suitable buffer, cooling quickly to 37°C, and allowing sufficient time for the polymerase to replicate both strands of the template. The temperature is then increased to 75°C to melt the newly formed duplexes and then cooled to 37°C. At the lower temperature more primer will anneal to initiate another round of replication. The heating-cooling cycle is repeated 20 to 30 times, after which the reaction products are fractionated on an agarose gel and photographed. The band containing the amplified fragment may be cut out of the gel and purified for further study. The DNA polymerase used in these reactions is isolated from thermophilic bacteria that can withstand temperatures of 70°C to 80°C. PCR applications are nearly limitless. It is used to amplify DNA from samples containing, at times, no more than a few cells. It can be used to screen libraries, and to identify genes that are turned on or off during embryonic development, or during cellular transformation.

The Human Genome Project

Sequencing the entire human genome is an idea that grew during a period of 20 years, beginning in the early 1980s. At that time, the DNA sequencing method invented by the British biochemist Fred Sanger, then at the University of Cambridge, was but a few years old and had only been used to sequence viral or mitochondrial genomes. (See chapter 8 for a description of sequencing methods.) Indeed, one of the first genomes to be sequenced was that of bacteriophage G4, a virus that infects the bacterium *E. coli*. The G4 genome consists of 5,577 nucleotide pairs (or base pairs, abbreviated bp) and was sequenced in Dr. Sanger's laboratory in 1979. By 1982 the Sanger protocol was used by others to sequence the genome of the animal virus SV40 (5,224 bp), the human mitochondrion (16,569 bp), and bacteriophage lambda (48,502 bp). Besides providing invaluable data, these projects demonstrated the feasibility of sequencing very large genomes.

The possibility of sequencing the entire human genome was first discussed at scientific meetings organized by the U.S. Department of Energy (DOE) between 1984 and 1986. A committee appointed by the U.S. National Research Council endorsed the idea in 1988 but recommended a broader program to include the sequencing of the genes of humans, bacteria, yeast, worms, flies, and mice. They also called for the establishment of research programs devoted to the ethical, legal, and social issues raised by human genome research. The program was formally launched in late 1990 as a consortium consisting of coordinated sequencing projects in the United States, Britain, France, Germany, Japan, and China. At about the same time, the Human Genome Organization (HUGO) was founded to provide a forum for international coordination of genomic research.

By 1995 the consortium had established a strategy called hierarchical shotgun sequencing that they applied to the human genome as well as to the other organisms mentioned. With this strategy, genomic DNA is cut into one-megabase (Mb) fragments (that is, each fragment consists of 1 million bases) that are cloned into bacterial artificial chromosomes (BACs) to form a library of DNA fragments. The BAC fragments are partially characterized, then organized into an overlapping assembly called a contig. Clones are selected from the contigs for shotgun sequencing. That is, each shotgun clone is digested into small 1,000 bp fragments, sequenced, and then assembled into the final sequence with the aid of computers. Organizing the initial BAC fragments into contigs greatly simplifies the final assembly stage.

Sequencing of the human genome was divided into two stages. The first stage, completed in 2001, was a rough draft that covered about 80 percent of the genome with an estimated size of more than 3 billion bases (also expressed as 3 gigabases, or 3 Gb). The final draft, completed in April 2003, covers the entire genome and refines the data for areas of the genome that were difficult to sequence. It also filled in many gaps that were present in the rough draft. The final draft of the human genome gives us a great deal of information that may be divided into three categories: gene content, gene origins, and gene organization.

GENE CONTENT

Analysis of the final draft has shown that the human genome consists of 3.2 Gb of DNA, which encodes about 30,000 genes (estimates range between 25,000 and 32,000). The estimated number of genes is surprisingly low; many scientists had believed the human genome contained 100,000 genes. By comparison, the fruit fly *Drosophila,* has 13,338 genes, and the simple underworm, *Caenorhabditis elegans,* has 18,266. The genome data suggests that human complexity, as compared to the fruit fly or the worm, is not simply due to the absolute number of genes, but involves the complexity of the proteins that are encoded by those genes. In general, human proteins tend to be much more complex than those of lower organisms. Data from the final draft and other sources provide a detailed overview of the functional profile of human cellular proteins.

GENE ORIGINS

Fully one-half of human genes originated as transposable elements, also known as jumping genes (these will be discussed at length in the following section). Equally surprising is the fact that 220 of our genes were obtained by horizontal transfer from bacteria, rather than ancestral, or vertical, inheritance. In other words, we obtained these genes directly from bacteria, probably during episodes of infection, in a kind of natural gene therapy, or gene swapping. We know this to be the case because while these genes occur in bacteria they are not present in yeast, fruit flies, or any other eukaryotes that have been tested.

The function of most of the horizontally transferred genes is unclear, although a few may code for basic metabolic enzymes. A notable exception is a gene that codes for an enzyme called monoamine oxidase (MAO). Monoamines are neurotransmitters, such as dopamine, norepinephrine, and serotonin, which are needed for neural signaling in the human central nervous system. Monoamine oxidase plays a crucial role in the turnover of these neurotransmitters. How MAO, obtained from bacteria, could have developed such an important role in human physiology is a great mystery.

GENE ORGANIZATION

In prokaryotes, genes are simply arranged in tandem along the chromosome, with little if any DNA separating one gene from the other. Each gene is transcribed into messenger RNA (mRNA), which is translated into protein. Indeed, in prokaryotes, which have no nucleus, translation often begins even before transcription is complete. In eukaryotes, as we might expect, gene organization is more complex. Data from the genome project shows clearly that eukaryote genes are split into subunits called exons, and that each exon is separated by a length of DNA called an intron. A gene consisting of introns and exons is separated from other genes by long stretches of noncoding DNA called intervening sequences. Eukaryote genes are transcribed into a primary RNA molecule that includes exon and intron sequences. The primary transcript never leaves the nucleus and is never translated into protein. Nuclear enzymes remove the introns from the primary transcript, after which the exons are joined together to form the mature mRNA. Thus, only the exons carry the necessary code to produce a protein.

X-Linked Severe Combined Immunodeficiency (SCID-X1)

The gene therapy trial for SCID-X1, conducted by Dr. Alain Fischer and his team at the Necker Hospital in Paris, France, is possibly the most important gene therapy trial to be launched since 1990. As introduced in chapter 5, this trial uses a combination of gene therapy and stem cell therapy to treat SCID-X1. This form of immunodeficiency is caused by a mutation in a gene that codes for the gamma chain (γC) of an interleukin receptor that occurs in the membranes of all lymphocytes (The gene for γC is referred to as γ_c). Interleukin receptors are dimeric or trimetric—that is, they consist of two or three polypeptide chains (β and γ, or, α, β, and γ) that span the cell membrane. The dimeric form is a receptor for IL4, IL7, IL9 and IL21. The trimeric form (known as IL2R) is a receptor for IL2 and IL15. Thus, a mutation in $γ_c$ destroys the cell's ability to receive signals from six interleukins. This not only interferes with the activation and mutation of T cells but also interferes with the normal development of NK cells and B cells. Consequently, children born with this defect are incapable of mounting an adaptive immune response.

Fischer's team developed a different protocol from that used in the DeSilva trial. Instead of transfecting isolated lymphocytes, they harvested stem cells from each patient's bone marrow. These cells are known as haematopoietic stem cells (HSCs). The HSCs were transfected in cell culture with a normal copy of the γc gene, carried by a retrovirus vector, and then reintroduced into the blood stream of the patient. The advantage of this approach is that the genetically corrected stem cells could reconstitute a healthy population of white blood cells and would continue doing so for the life of the patient. In the case of the DeSilva trial, lymphocytes were transfected and reintroduced into the patient's blood stream, but once these genetically corrected cells had died, they were replaced by defective lymphocytes, because the patient's stem cells had not been corrected. Thus, in a case of the DeSilva trial, genetically corrected lymphocytes had to be reintroduced at regular intervals in order to maintain a functional immune system.

Fischer's team treated 10 patients, all of whom showed a dramatic improvement in their immune response that was characterized by an increase in the number of T, B, and NK cells. The overall profile of the patients' immune system, with regard to the number and function of the lymphocytes, was shown to be similar to that of age-matched controls. However, in January 2003, two of the subjects were diagnosed with T cell leukemia and, by the end of that year, researchers had determined that the cancerous cells could be traced to the genetically modified stem cells. It was also shown that the retrovirus used in the trial caused the cancers by inserting within or near an oncogene known as *LMO2*.

Immediately after the cancer cases were diagnosed, regulatory agencies in Europe and the United States stopped all gene therapy trials that were using retroviral vectors. In March 2003, the U.S. Food and Drug

Administration (FDA) and equivalent European agencies agreed to lift the ban after carefully considering the following points: first, the majority of the children in the Fischer trial showed major improvements in their overall health and are now able to live normal lives; second, the complication of leukemia has not occurred in any of the more than 250 patients currently enrolled in more than 40 clinical trials involving retroviral vectors; and, finally, the incidence of adverse effects was deemed to be too low to justify cessation of other retroviral gene transfer studies. As of June 2004, the two patients who developed cancer in the Fischer trial were undergoing treatment and were doing well.

When the Fischer trial began, in 1998, most scientists did not consider the possibility of cancers being induced by the vector. The main concern was to avoid the kind of complications that arose during the Gelsinger Trial. However, it is now clear that insertional mutagenesis caused by the vector is a very serious problem that needs to be overcome before gene therapy can become a practical reality. In 2004, scientists in the United States and Europe began identifying all retroviral integration sites (RISs) in the human and mouse genomes (determination of RISs in the mouse genome is important for preclinical research). This search is conducted by transfecting cells in culture and then, using PCR and other methods, mapping out the chromosomal location of the RIS and the exact sequence around the insertion site. This information will make it possible to identify or design vectors that can be inserted in gene-poor regions, far away from any known oncogenes.

Alzheimer's Disease (AD)

In April 2004, a research team at the University of California, San Diego, headed by Dr. Mark Tuszynski, reported some success in a Phase I clinical trial to treat AD. Tuszynski's team began by isolating skin cells from each of eight patients recruited for the study and transfected those cells with a vector carrying a gene coding for nerve growth factor (NGF). In preclinical studies, other researchers have shown that NGF, a protein, appears to help neurons resist the kind of degeneration that is typical of AD. The genetically modified skin cells were injected into the brains of the eight patients. Because each patient received an injection of his or her own genetically modified cells, immune rejection was not a problem. One year later, the patients' rate of mental decline was reduced by half. By comparison, currently available drug therapies reduce mental decline by only 5 percent. Tuszynski's team is currently preparing to launch a larger follow-up study to confirm these results.

Huntingdon's Disease (HD)

The neurological damage caused by HD is due to the buildup of the mutant Huntingdon protein. Researchers have reasoned that even without correcting the gene, it could be possible to treat this disease by blocking the synthesis of the protein by deactivating the mRNA. In June 2004, Dr. Beverly Davidson at the University of Iowa reported the results of a preclinical study in mice that involved a disorder similar to HD, known as spinocerebellar ataxia, which affects the animal's ability to walk. Davidson's team produced a vector containing a therapeutic DNA molecule that had a base sequence complementary to the ataxia mRNA. In vivo hybridization between the mRNA and the therapeutic DNA was expected to block the translation of the mRNA. This form of gene therapy is known as RNA interference. After injecting the vector into the mice, Davidson's team found that the production of the defective protein was indeed blocked and the mice seemed to improve. They also tested their procedure on human cells in culture, where they were able to block the production of the Huntingdon's protein. Davidson is now planning to test this very promising procedure in a Phase I human trial.

GLOSSARY

✕

acetyl A chemical group derived from acetic acid. Important in energy metabolism and for the modification of proteins.

acetylcholine A neurotransmitter released at axonal terminals by cholinergic neurons. Found in the central and peripheral nervous system and released at the vertebrate neuromuscular junction.

acetyl-CoA A water-soluble molecule, coenzyme A (CoA), that carries acetyl groups in cells.

acid A substance that releases protons when dissolved in water. Carries a net negative charge.

actin filament A protein filament formed by the polymerization of globular actin molecules. Forms the cytoskeleton of all eukaryotes and part of the contractile apparatus of skeletal muscle.

action potential A self-propagating electrical impulse that occurs in the membranes of neurons, muscles, photoreceptors, and hair cells of the inner ear.

active transport Movement of molecules across the cell membrane, utilizing the energy stored in ATP.

adenylate cyclase A membrane-bound enzyme that catalyzes the conversion of ATP to cyclic AMP. An important component of cell-signaling pathways.

adherens junction A cell junction in which the cytoplasmic face of the membrane is attached to actin filaments.

adipocyte A fat cell.

adrenaline (epinephrine) A hormone released by chromaffin cells in the adrenal gland. Prepares an animal for extreme activity, increases the heart rate and blood-sugar levels.

adult stem cells Stem cells isolated from adult tissues, such as bone marrow or epithelium.

aerobic   Refers to a process that either requires oxygen or occurs in its presence.

allele   An alternate form of a gene. Diploid organisms have two alleles for each gene, located at the same locus (position) on homologous chromosomes.

allogeneic transplant   A patient receives a tissue or organ transplant from an unrelated individual.

alpha helix   A common folding pattern of proteins in which a linear sequence of amino acids twists into a right-handed helix stabilized by hydrogen bonds.

amino acid   An organic molecule containing amino and carboxyl groups that is a building block of protein.

aminoacyl tRNA   An amino acid linked by its carboxyl group to a hydroxyl group on tRNA.

aminoacyl-tRNA synthetase   An enzyme that attaches the correct amino acid to a tRNA.

amino terminus   The end of a protein or polypeptide chain that carries a free amino group.

amphipathic   Having both hydrophilic and hydrophobic regions, as in a phospholipid.

anabolism   A collection of metabolic reactions in a cell whereby large molecules are made from smaller ones.

anaerobic   A cellular metabolism that does not depend on molecular oxygen.

anaphase   A mitotic stage in which the two sets of chromosomes move away from each other toward opposite and spindle poles.

anchoring junction   A cell junction that attaches cells to each other.

angiogenesis   Sprouting of new blood vessels from preexisting ones.

angstrom   A unit of length, equal to 10^{-10} meter or 0.1 nanometer (nm), that is used to measure molecules and atoms.

anterior   A position close to or at the head end of the body.

antibiotic   A substance made by bacteria, fungi, and plants that is toxic to microorganisms. Common examples are penicillin and streptomycin.

antibody   A protein made by B cells of the immune system in response to invading microbes.

anticodon   A sequence of three nucleotides in tRNA that is complementary to a messenger RNA codon.

antigen   A molecule that stimulates an immune response, leading to the formation of antibodies.

antigen-presenting cell   A cell of the immune system, such as a monocyte, that presents pieces of an invading microbe (the antigen) to lymphocytes.

antiparallel   The relative orientation of the two strands in a DNA double helix; the polarity of one strand is oriented in the opposite direction to the other.

antiporter   A membrane carrier protein that transports two different molecules across a membrane in opposite directions.

apoptosis   Regulated or programmed form of cell death that may be activated by the cell itself or by the immune system to force cells to commit suicide when they become infected with a virus.

asexual reproduction   The process of forming new individuals without gametes or the fertilization of an egg by a sperm. Individuals produced this way are identical to the parent and referred to as a clone.

aster   The star-shaped arrangement of microtubules that is characteristic of a mitotic or meiotic spindle.

ATP (adenosine triphosphate)   A nucleoside consisting of adenine, ribose, and three phosphate groups that is the main carrier of chemical energy in the cell.

ATPase   Any enzyme that catalyzes a biochemical reaction by extracting the necessary energy from ATP.

ATP synthase   A protein located in the inner membrane of the mitochondrion that catalyzes the formation of ATP from ADP and inorganic phosphate using the energy supplied by the electron transport chain.

autogeneic transplant   A patient receives a transplant of his or her own tissue.

autosome   Any chromosome other than a sex chromosome.

axon   A long extension of a neuron's cell body that transmits an electrical signal to other neurons.

axonal transport   The transport of organelles, such as Golgi vesicles, along an axon to the axonal terminus. Transport also flows from the terminus to the cell body.

bacteria   One of the most ancient forms of cellular life (the other is the Archaea). Bacteria are prokaryotes and some are known to cause disease.

bacterial artificial chromosome (BAC)   A cloning vector that accommodates DNA inserts of up to 1 million base pairs.

bacteriophage   A virus that infects bacteria. Bacteriophages were used to prove that DNA is the cell's genetic material and are now used as cloning vectors.

base   A substance that can accept a proton in solution. The purines and pyrimidines in DNA and RNA are organic bases and are often referred to simply as bases.

base pair   Two nucleotides in RNA or DNA that are held together by hydrogen bonds. Adenine bound to thymine or guanine bound to cytosine are examples of base pairs.

B cell (B lymphocyte)   A white blood cell that makes antibodies and is part of the adaptive immune response.

benign   Tumors that grow to a limited size and do not spread to other parts of the body.

beta sheet   Common structural motif in proteins in which different strands of the protein run alongside each other and are held together by hydrogen bonds.

biopsy   The removal of cells or tissues for examination under a microscope. When only a sample of tissue is removed, the procedure is called an incisional biopsy or core biopsy. When an entire lump or suspicious area is removed, the procedure is called an excisional biopsy. When a sample of tissue or fluid is removed with a needle, the procedure is called a needle biopsy or fine-needle aspiration.

biosphere   The world of living organisms.

bivalent   A duplicated chromosome paired with its homologous duplicated chromosome at the beginning of meiosis.

blastomere   A cell formed by the cleavage of a fertilized egg. Blastomeres are the totipotent cells of the early embryo.

blotting   A technique for transferring DNA (Southern blotting), RNA (northern blotting), or proteins (western blotting) from an agarose or polyacrylamide gel to a nylon membrane.

BRCA1 (breast cancer gene 1)   A gene on chromosome 17 that may be involved in regulating the cell cycle. A person who inherits an altered version of the BRCA1 gene has a higher risk of getting breast, ovarian, or prostate cancer.

BRCA2 (breast cancer gene 2) A gene on chromosome 13 that, when mutated, increases the risk of getting breast, ovarian, or prostate cancer.

budding yeast The common name for the baker's yeast *Saccharomyces cerevisiae,* a popular experimental organism that reproduces by budding off a parental cell.

cadherin Belongs to a family of proteins that mediates cell-to-cell adhesion in animal tissues.

calorie A unit of heat. One calorie is the amount of heat needed to raise the temperature of one gram of water by 1°C. Kilocalories (1,000 calories) are used to describe the energy content of foods.

capsid The protein coat of a virus, formed by auto-assembly of one or more proteins into a geometrically symmetrical structure.

carbohydrate A general class of compounds that includes sugars, containing carbon, hydrogen, and oxygen.

carboxyl group A carbon atom attached to an oxygen and a hydroxyl group.

carboxyl terminus The end of a protein containing a carboxyl group.

carcinogen A compound or form of radiation that can cause cancer.

carcinogenesis The formation of a cancer.

carcinoma Cancer of the epithelium, representing the majority of human cancers.

cardiac muscle Muscle of the heart. Composed of myocytes that are linked together in a communication network based on free passage of small molecules through gap junctions.

caspase A protease involved in the initiation of apoptosis.

catabolism Enzyme-regulated breakdown of large molecules for the extraction of chemical-bond energy. Intermediate products are called catabolites.

catalyst A substance that lowers the activation energy of a reaction.

CD28 Cell-surface protein located in T cell membranes, necessary for the activation of T cells by foreign antigens.

cDNA (complementary DNA) DNA that is synthesized from mRNA, thus containing the complementary sequence. cDNA contains coding sequence but not the regulatory sequences that are present in the genome. Labeled probes are made from cDNA for the study of gene expression.

cell adhesion molecule (CAM)   A cell surface protein that is used to connect cells to each other.

cell body   The main part of a cell containing the nucleus, Golgi complex, and endoplasmic reticulum. Used in reference to neurons that have long processes (dendrites and axons) extending some distance from the nucleus and cytoplasmic machinery.

cell coat   See **glycocalyx**.

cell-cycle control system   A team of regulatory proteins that governs progression through the cell cycle.

cell-division-cycle gene (*cdc* gene)   A gene that controls a specific step in the cell cycle.

cell fate   The final differentiated state that a pluripotent embryonic cell is expected to attain.

cell-medicated immune response   Activation of specific cells to launch an immune response against an invading microbe.

cell nuclear replacement   Animal-cloning technique whereby a somatic cell nucleus is transferred to an enucleated oocyte. Synonomous with somatic-cell nuclear transfer.

central nervous system (CNS)   That part of a nervous system that analyzes signals from the body and the environment. In animals, the CNS includes the brain and spinal cord.

centriole   A cylindrical array of microtubules that is found at the center of a centrosome in animal cells.

centromere   A region of a mitotic chromosome that holds sister chromatids together. Microtubules of the spindle fiber connect to an area of the centromere called the kinetochore.

centrosome   Organizes the mitotic spindle and the spindle poles. In most animal cells it contains a pair of centrioles.

chiasma (plural: chiasmata)   An X-shaped connection between homologous chromosomes that occurs during meiosis I, representing a site of crossing-over, or genetic exchange between the two chromosomes.

chromatid   A duplicate chromosome that is still connected to the original at the centromere. The identical pair are called sister chromatids.

chromatin A complex of DNA and proteins (histones and nonhistones) that forms each chromosome and is found in the nucleus of all eukaryotes. Decondensed and threadlike during interphase.

chromatin condensation Compaction of different regions of interphase chromosomes that is mediated by the histones.

chromosome One long molecule of DNA that contains the organism's genes. In prokaryotes, the chromosome is circular and naked; in eukaryotes, it is linear and complexed with histone and nonhistone proteins.

chromosome condensation Compaction of entire chromosomes in preparation for cell division.

clinical breast exam An exam of the breast performed by a physician to check for lumps or other changes.

cyclic adenosine monophosphate (cAMP) A second messenger in a cell-signaling pathway that is produced from ATP by the enzyme adenylate cyclase.

cyclin A protein that activates protein kinases (cyclin-dependent protein kinases, or Cdk) that control progression from one state of the cell cycle to another.

cytochemistry The study of the intracellular distribution of chemicals.

cytochrome Colored, iron-containing protein that is part of the electron transport chain.

cytotoxic T cell A T lymphocyte that kills infected body cells.

dendrite An extension of a nerve cell that receives signals from other neurons.

dexrazoxane A drug used to protect the heart from the toxic effects of anthracycline drugs such as doxorubicin. It belongs to the family of drugs called chemoprotective agents.

dideoxy sequencing A method for sequencing DNA that employs dideoxyribose nucleotides.

diploid A genetic term meaning two sets of homologous chromosomes, one set from the mother and the other from the father. Thus diploid organisms have two versions (alleles) of each gene in the genome.

DNA (deoxyribonucleic acid) A long polymer formed by linking four different kinds of nucleotides together like beads on a string. The sequence of nucleotides is used to encode an organism's genes.

DNA helicase   An enzyme that separates and unwinds the two DNA strands in preparation for replication or transcription.

DNA library   A collection of DNA fragments that are cloned into plasmids or viral genomes.

DNA ligase   An enzyme that joins two DNA strands together to make a continuous DNA molecule.

DNA microarray   A technique for studying the simultaneous expression of a very large number of genes.

DNA polymerase   An enzyme that synthesizes DNA using one strand as a template.

DNA primase   An enzyme that synthesizes a short strand of RNA that serves as a primer for DNA replication.

dorsal   The backside of an animal. Also refers to the upper surface of anatomical structures, such as arms or wings.

dorsoventral   The body axis running from the backside to the frontside or the upperside to the underside of a structure.

double helix   The three-dimensional structure of DNA in which the two strands twist around each other to form a spiral.

doxorubicin   An anticancer drug that belongs to a family of antitumor antibiotics.

Drosophila melanogaster   Small species of fly, commonly called a fruit fly, that is used as an experimental organism in genetics, embryology, and gerontology.

ductal carcinoma in situ (DCIS)   Abnormal cells that involve only the lining of a breast duct. The cells have not spread outside the duct to other tissues in the breast. Also called intraductal carcinoma.

dynein   A motor protein that is involved in chromosome movements during cell division.

dysplasia   Disordered growth of cells in a tissue or organ, often leading to the development of cancer.

ectoderm   An embryonic tissue that is the precursor of the epidermis and the nervous system.

electrochemical gradient   A differential concentration of an ion or molecule across the cell membrane that serves as a source of potential energy and may polarize the cell electrically.

electron microscope   A microscope that uses electrons to produce a high-resolution image of the cell.

embryogensis   The development of an embryo from a fertilized egg.

embryonic stem cell (ES cell)   A pluripotent cell derived from the inner cell mass (the cells that give rise to the embryo instead of the placenta) of a mammalian embryo.

endocrine cell   A cell that is specialized for the production and release of hormones. Such cells make up hormone-producing tissue such as the pituitary gland or gonads.

endocytosis   Cellular uptake of material from the environment by invagination of the cell membrane to form a vesicle called an endosome. The endosome's contents are made available to the cell after it fuses with a lysosome.

endoderm   An embryonic tissue layer that gives rise to the gut.

endoplasmic reticulum (ER)   Membrane-bounded chambers that are used to modify newly synthesized proteins with the addition of sugar molecules (glycosylation). When finished, the glycosylated proteins are sent to the Golgi apparatus in exocytotic vesicles.

endothelial cell   A cell that forms the endothelium, a thin sheet of cells lining the inner surface of all blood vessels.

enhancer   A DNA regulatory sequence that provides a binding site for transcription factors capable of increasing the rate of transcription for a specific gene. Often located thousands of base pairs away from the gene it regulates.

enveloped virus   A virus containing a capsid that is surrounded by a lipid bilayer originally obtained from the membrane of a previously infected cell.

enzyme   A protein or RNA that catalyzes a specific chemical reaction.

epidermis   The epithelial layer, or skin, that covers the outer surface of the body.

ER signal sequence   The amino terminal sequence that directs proteins to enter the endoplasmic reticulum (ER). This sequence is removed once the protein enters the ER.

erythrocyte   A red blood cell that contains the oxygen-carrying pigment hemoglobin used to deliver oxygen to cells in the body.

Escherichia coli (*E. coli*)   Rod shape, gram negative bacterium that inhabits the intestinal tract of most animals and is used as an experimental organism by geneticists and biomedical researchers.

eukaryote (eucaryote)   A cell containing a nucleus and many membrane-bounded organelles. All life-forms, except bacteria and viruses, are composed of eukaryote cells.

euchromatin   Lightly staining portion of interphase chromatin, in contrast to the darkly staining heterochromatin (condensed chromatin). Euchromatin contains most, if not all, of the active genes.

exocytosis   The process by which molecules are secreted from a cell. Molecules to be secreted are located in Golgi-derived vesicles that fuse with the inner surface of the cell membrane, depositing the contents into the intercellular space.

exon   Coding region of a eukaryote gene that is represented in messenger RNA, and thus directs the synthesis of a specific protein.

expression studies   Examination of the type and quantity of mRNA or protein that is produced by cells, tissues, or organs.

fat   A lipid material, consisting of triglycerides (fatty acids bound to glycerol), that is stored in adipocytes as an energy reserve.

fatty acid   A compound that has a carboxylic acid attached to a long hydrocarbon chain. A major source of cellular energy and a component of phospholipids.

filter hybridization   The detection of specific DNA or RNA molecules, fixed on a nylon filter, by incubating the filter with a labelled probe that hybridizes to the target sequence.

fertilization   The fusion of haploid male and female gametes to form a diploid zygote.

fibroblast   The cell type that, by secreting an extracellular matrix, gives rise to the connective tissue of the body.

fixative   A chemical that is used to preserve cells and tissues. Common examples are formaldehyde, methanol, and acetic acid.

flagellum (plural: flagella)   Whiplike structure found in prokaryotes and eukaryotes that are used to propel cells through water.

fluorescein   Fluorescent dye that produces a green light when illuminated with ultraviolet or blue light.

fluorescent microscope   A microscope that is equipped with special filters and a beam splitter for the examination of tissues and cells stained with a fluorescent dye.

fluorescent dye   A dye that absorbs UV or blue light and emits light of a longer wavelength, usually as green or red light.

follicle cell Cells that surround and help feed a developing oocyte.

G_0 G "zero" refers to a phase of the cell cycle. State of withdrawal from the cycle as the cell enters a resting or quiescent stage. Occurs in differentiated body cells as well as developing oocytes.

G_1 Gap 1 refers to the phase of the cell cycle that occurs just after mitosis and before the next round of DNA synthesis.

G_2 The Gap 2 phase of the cell cycle follows DNA replication and precedes mitosis.

gap junction A communication channel in the membranes of adjacent cells that allows free passage of ions and small molecules.

gastrulation An embryological event in which a spherical embryo is converted into an elongated structure with a head end, a tail end, and a gut (gastrula).

gene A region of the DNA that specifies a specific protein or RNA molecule that is handed down from one generation to the next. This region includes both the coding, noncoding, and regulatory sequences.

gene regulatory protein Any protein that binds to DNA and thereby affects the expression of a specific gene.

gene repressor protein A protein that binds to DNA and blocks transcription of a specific gene.

gene therapy A method for treating disease whereby a defective gene, causing the disease, is either repaired, replaced, or supplemented with a functional copy.

genetic code A set of rules that assigns a specific DNA or RNA triplet, consisting of a three-base sequence, to a specific amino acid.

genome All of the genes that belong to a cell or an organism.

genomic library A collection of DNA fragments, obtained by digesting genomic DNA with a restriction enzyme, that are cloned into plasmid or viral vectors.

genomics The study of DNA sequences and their role in the function and structure of an organism.

genotype The genetic composition of a cell or organism.

germ cell Cells that develop into gametes, either sperm or oocytes.

glucose Six-carbon monosaccharide (sugar) that is the principal source of energy for many cells and organisms. Stored as glycogen in animal cells and as starch in plants. Wood is an elaborate polymer of glucose and other sugars.

glycerol   A three-carbon alcohol that is an important component of phospholipids.

glycocalyx   A molecular "forest," consisting of glycosylated proteins and lipids, that covers the surface of every cell. The glycoproteins and glycolipids, carried to the cell membrane by Golgi-derived vesicles, have many functions, including the formation of ion channels, cell-signaling receptors and transporters.

glycogen   A polymer of glucose used to store energy in an animal cell.

glycolysis   The degradation of glucose with production of ATP.

glycoprotein   Any protein that has a chain of glucose molecules (oligosaccharide) attached to some of the amino acid residues.

glycosylation   The process of adding one or more sugar molecules to proteins or lipids.

glycosyl transferase   An enzyme in the Golgi complex that adds glucose to proteins.

Golgi complex (Golgi apparatus)   Membrane-bounded organelle in eukaryote cells that receives glycoproteins from the ER, which are modified and sorted before being sent to their final destination. The Golgi complex is also the source of glycolipids that are destined for the cell membrane. The glycoproteins and glycolipids leave the Golgi by exocytosis. This organelle is named after the Italian histologist Camillo Golgi, who discovered it in 1898.

granulocyte   A type of white blood cell that includes the neutrophils, basophils, and eosinophils.

growth factor   A small protein (polypeptide) that can stimulate cells to grow and proliferate.

haploid   Having only one set of chromosomes. A condition that is typical in gametes, such as sperm and eggs.

HeLa cell   A tumor-derived cell line, originally isolated from a cancer patient in 1951. Currently used by many laboratories to study the cell biology of cancer and carcinogenesis.

helix-loop-helix   A structural motif common to a group of gene regulatory proteins.

helper T cell   A type of T lymphocyte that helps stimulate B cells to make antibodies directed against a specific microbe or antigen.

hemoglobin An iron-containing protein complex, located in red blood cells that picks up oxygen in the lungs and carries it to other tissues and cells of the body.

hemopoiesis Production of blood cells, occurring primarily in the bone marrow.

hepatocyte A liver cell.

heterochromatin A region of a chromosome that is highly condensed and transcriptionally inactive.

histochemistry The study of chemical differentiation of tissues.

histology The study of tissues.

histone Small nuclear proteins, rich in the amino acids arginine and lysine, that form the nucleosome in eukaryote nuclei, a beadlike structure that is a major component of chromatin.

HIV The human immunodeficiency virus that is responsible for AIDS.

homolog One of two or more genes that have a similar sequence and are descended from a common ancestor gene.

homologous Organs or molecules that are similar in structure because they have descended from a common ancestor. Used primarily in reference to DNA and protein sequences.

homologous chromosomes Two copies of the same chromosome, one inherited from the mother and the other from the father.

hormone A signaling molecule, produced and secreted by endocrine glands. Usually released into general circulation for coordination of an animal's physiology.

housekeeping gene A gene that codes for a protein that is needed by all cells, regardless of the cell's specialization. Genes encoding enzymes involved in glycolysis and the Krebs cycle are common examples.

hybridization A term used in molecular biology (recombinant DNA technology) meaning the formation of a double-stranded nucleic acid through complementary base-pairing. A property that is exploited in filter hybridization, a procedure that is used to screen gene libraries and to study gene structure and expression.

hydrophilic A polar compound that mixes readily with water.

hydrophobic A nonpolar molecule that dissolves in fat and lipid solutions but not in water.

hydroxyl group (-OH) Chemical group consisting of oxygen and hydrogen that is a prominent part of alcohol.

image analysis A computerized method for extracting information from digitized microscopic images of cells or cell organelles.

immunofluorescence Detection of a specific cellular protein with the aid of a fluorescent dye that is coupled to an antibody.

immunoglobulin (Ig) An antibody made by B cells as part of the adaptive immune response.

incontinence Inability to control the flow of urine from the bladder (urinary incontinence) or the escape of stool from the rectum (fecal incontinence).

in situ hybridization A method for studying gene expression, whereby a labeled cDNA or RNA probe hybridizes to a specific mRNA in intact cells or tissues. The procedure is usually carried out on tissue sections or smears of individual cells.

insulin Polypeptide hormone secreted by β (beta) cells in the vertebrate pancreas. Production of this hormone is regulated directly by the amount of glucose that is in the blood.

interleukin A small protein hormone, secreted by lymphocytes, to activate and coordinate the adaptive immune response.

interphase The period between each cell division, which includes the G_1, S, and G_2 phases of the cell cycle.

intron A section of a eukaryote gene that is non-coding. It is transcribed, but does not appear in the mature mRNA.

in vitro Refers to cells growing in culture, or a biochemical reaction occurring in a test tube (Latin for "in glass").

in vivo A biochemical reaction, or a process, occurring in living cells or a living organism (Latin for "in life").

ion An atom that has gained or lost electrons, thus acquiring a charge. Common examples are Na^+ and Ca^{++} ions.

ion channel A transmembrane channel that allows ions to diffuse across the membrane and down their electrochemical gradient.

Jak-STAT signaling pathway One of several cell-signaling pathways that activates gene expression. The pathway is activated through cell-surface receptors and cytoplasmic Janus kinases (Jaks), and signal transducers and activators of transcription (STATs).

karyotype   A pictorial catalog of a cell's chromosomes, showing their number, size, shape, and overall banding pattern.

keratin   Proteins produced by specialized epithelial cells called keratinocytes. Keratin is found in hair, fingernails, and feathers.

kinesin   A motor protein that uses energy obtained from the hydrolysis of ATP to move along a microtubule.

kinetochore   A complex of proteins that forms around the centromere of mitotic or meiotic chromosomes, providing an attachment site for microtubules. The other end of each microtubule is attached to a chromosome.

Krebs cycle (citric acid cycle)   The central metabolic pathway in all eukaryotes and aerobic prokaryotes, discovered by the German chemist Hans Krebs in 1937. The cycle oxidizes acetyl groups derived from food molecules. The end products are CO_2, H_2O, and high-energy electrons, which pass via NADH and FADH2 to the respiratory chain. In eukaryotes, the Krebs cycle is located in the mitochondria.

labeling reaction   The addition of a radioactive atom or fluorescent dye to DNA or RNA for use as a probe in filter hybridization.

lagging strand   One of the two newly synthesized DNA strands at a replication fork. The lagging strand is synthesized discontinuously, and therefore, its completion lags behind the second, or leading, strand.

lambda bacteriophage   A viral parasite that infects bacteria. Widely used as a DNA cloning vector.

leading strand   One of the two newly synthesized DNA strands at a replication fork. The leading strand is made by continuous synthesis in the 5' to 3' direction.

leucine zipper   A structural motif of DNA binding proteins, in which two identical proteins are joined together at regularly spaced leucine residues, much like a zipper, to form a dimer.

leukemia   Cancer of white blood cells.

lipid bilayer   Two closely aligned sheets of phospholipids that form the core structure of all cell membranes. The two layers are aligned such that the hydrophobic tails are interior, while the hydrophilic head groups are exterior on both surfaces.

liposome   An artificial lipid bilayer vesicle used in membrane studies and as an artificial gene therapy vector.

locus   A term from genetics that refers to the position of a gene along a chromosome. Different alleles of the same gene occupy the same locus.

long-term potentiation (LTP)   A physical remodeling of synaptic junctions that receive continuous stimulation.

lymphocyte   A type of white blood cell that is involved in the adaptive immune response. There are two kinds of lymphocytes: T lymphocytes and B lymphocytes. T lymphocytes (T cells) mature in the thymus and attack invading microbes directly. B lymphocytes (B cells) mature in the bone marrow and make antibodies that are designed to immobilize or destroy specific microbes or antigens.

lysis   The rupture of the cell membrane followed by death of the cell.

lysosome   Membrane-bounded organelle of eukaryotes that contains powerful digestive enzymes.

macromolecule   A very large molecule that is built from smaller molecular subunits. Common examples are DNA, proteins, and polysaccharides.

magnetic resonance imaging (MRI)   A procedure in which radio waves and a powerful magnet linked to a computer are used to create detailed pictures of areas inside the body. These pictures can show the difference between normal and diseased tissue. MRI makes better images of organs and soft tissue than other scanning techniques, such as CT or X-ray. MRI is especially useful for imaging the brain, spine, the soft tissue of joints, and the inside of bones. Also called nuclear magnetic resonance imaging.

major histocompatibility complex   Vertebrate genes that code for a large family of cell-surface glycoproteins that bind foreign antigens and present them to T cells to induce an immune response.

malignant   Refers to the functional status of a cancer cell that grows aggressively and is able to metastasize, or colonize, other areas of the body.

mammography   The use of X-rays to create a picture of the breast.

MAP-kinase (mitogen-activated protein kinase)   A protein kinase that is part of a cell-proliferation-inducing signaling pathway.

M-cyclin   A eukaryote enzyme that regulates mitosis.

meiosis   A special form of cell division by which haploid gametes are produced. This is accomplished with two rounds of cell division but only one round of DNA replication.

melanocyte   A skin cell that produces the pigment melanin.

membrane   The lipid bilayer, and the associated glycocalyx, that surrounds and encloses all cells.

membrane channel   A protein complex that forms a pore or channel through the membrane for the free passage of ions and small molecules.

membrane potential   A buildup of charged ions on one side of the cell membrane establishes an electrochemical gradient that is measured in millivolts (mV). An important characteristic of neurons as it provides the electric current, when ion channels open, that enable these cells to communicate with each other.

mesoderm   An embryonic germ layer that gives rise to muscle, connective tissue, bones, and many internal organs.

messenger RNA (mRNA)   An RNA transcribed from a gene that is used as the gene template by the ribosomes, and other components of the translation machinery, to synthesize a protein.

metabolism   The sum total of the chemical processes that occur in living cells.

metaphase   The stage of mitosis at which the chromosomes are attached to the spindle but have not begun to move apart.

metaphase plate   Refers to the imaginary plane established by the chromosomes as they line up at right angles to the spindle poles.

metaplasia   A change in the pattern of cellular behavior that often precedes the development of cancer.

metastasis   Spread of cancer cells from the site of the original tumor to other parts of the body.

methyl group (-CH$_3$)   Hydrophobic chemical group derived from methane. Occurs at the end of a fatty acid.

micrograph   Photograph taken through a light, or electron, microscope.

micrometer (μm or micron)   Equal to 10^{-6} meters.

microtubule   A fine cylindrical tube made of the protein tubulin, forming a major component of the eukaryote cytoskeleton.

millimeter (mm)   Equal to 10^{-3} meters.

mitochondrion (plural: mitochondria) Eukaryote organelle, formerly free-living, that produces most of the cell's ATP.

mitogen A hormone or signaling molecule that stimulates cells to grow and divide.

mitosis Division of a eukaryotic nucleus. From the Greek *mitos,* meaning "a thread," in reference to the threadlike appearance of interphase chromosomes.

mitotic chromosome Highly condensed duplicated chromosomes held together by the centromere. Each member of the pair is referred to as a sister chromatid.

mitotic spindle Array of microtubules, fanning out from the polar centrioles and connecting to each of the chromosomes.

molecule Two or more atoms linked together by covalent bonds.

monoclonal antibody An antibody produced from a B cell–derived clonal line. Since all of the cells are clones of the original B cell, the antibodies produced are identical.

monocyte A type of white blood cell that is involved in the immune response.

motif An element of structure or pattern that may be a recurring domain in a variety of proteins.

M phase The period of the cell cycle (mitosis or meiosis) when the chromosomes separate and migrate to the opposite poles of the spindle.

multipass transmembrane protein A membrane protein that passes back and forth across the lipid bilayer.

mutant A genetic variation within a population.

mutation A heritable change in the nucleotide sequence of a chromosome.

myelin sheath Insulation applied to the axons of neurons. The sheath is produced by oligodendrocytes in the central nervous system and by Schwann cells in the peripheral nervous system.

myeloid cell White blood cells other than lymphocytes.

myoblast Muscle precursor cell. Many myoblasts fuse into a syncytium, containing many nuclei, to form a single muscle cell.

myocyte A muscle cell.

NAD (nicotine adenine dinucleotide) Accepts a hydride ion (H^-), produced by the Krebs cycle, forming NADH, the main carrier of electrons for oxidative phosphorylation.

NADH dehydrogenase Removes electrons from NADH and passes them down the electron transport chain.

nanometer (nm) Equal to 10^{-9} meters or 10^{-3} microns.

natural killer cell (NK cell) A lymphocyte that kills virus-infected cells in the body. They also kill foreign cells associated with a tissue or organ transplant.

neuromuscular junction A special form of synapse between a motor neuron and a skeletal muscle cell.

neuron A cell specially adapted for communication that forms the nervous system of all animals.

neurotransmitter A chemical released by neurons at a synapse that transmits a signal to another neuron.

non-small-cell lung cancer A group of lung cancers that includes squamous cell carcinoma, adenocarcinoma, and large cell carcinoma. The small cells are endocrine cells.

northern blotting A technique for the study of gene expression. Messenger RNA (mRNA) is fractionated on an agarose gel and then transferred to a piece of nylon filter paper (or membrane). A specific mRNA is detected by hybridization with a labeled DNA or RNA probe. The original blotting technique invented by E. M. Southern inspired the name.

nuclear envelope The double membrane (two lipid bilayers) enclosing the cell nucleus.

nuclear localization signal (NLS) A short amino acid sequence located on proteins that are destined for the cell nucleus after they are translated in the cytoplasm.

nucleic acid DNA or RNA, a macromolecule consisting of a chain of nucleotides.

nucleolar organizer Region of a chromosome containing a cluster of ribosomal RNA genes that gives rise to the nucleolus.

nucleolus A structure in the nucleus where ribosomal RNA is transcribed and ribosomal subunits are assembled.

nucleoside A purine or pyrimidine linked to a ribose or deoxyribose sugar.

nucleosome A beadlike structure, consisting of histone proteins.

nucleotide A nucleoside containing one or more phosphate groups linked to the 5' carbon of the ribose sugar. DNA and RNA are nucleotide polymers.

nucleus   Eukaryote cell organelle that contains the DNA genome on one or more chromosomes.

oligodendrocyte   A myelinating glia cell of the vertebrate central nervous system.

oligo labeling   A method for incorporating labeled nucleotides into a short piece of DNA or RNA. Also known as the random-primer labeling method.

oligomer   A short polymer, usually consisting of amino acids (oligopeptides), sugars (oligosaccharides), or nucleotides (oligonucleotides). Taken from the Greek word *oligos,* meaning "few" or "little."

oncogene   A mutant form of a normal cellular gene, known as a proto-oncogene, that can transform a cell to a cancerous phenotype.

oocyte   A female gamete or egg cell.

operator   A region of a prokaryote chromosome that controls the expression of adjacent genes.

operon   Two or more prokaryote genes that are transcribed into a single mRNA.

organelle   A membrane-bounded structure, occurring in eukaryote cells, that has a specialized function. Examples are the nucleus, Golgi complex, and endoplasmic reticulum.

osmosis   The movement of solvent across a semipermeable membrane that separates a solution with a high concentration of solutes from one with a low concentration of solutes. The membrane must be permeable to the solvent but not to the solutes. In the context of cellular osmosis, the solvent is always water, the solutes are ions and molecules, and the membrane is the cell membrane.

osteoblast   Cells that form bones.

ovulation   Rupture of a mature follicle with subsequent release of a mature oocyte from the ovary.

oxidative phosphorylation   Generation of high-energy electrons from food molecules that are used to power the synthesis of ATP from ADP and inorganic phosphate. The electrons are eventually transferred to oxygen to complete the process. Occurs in bacteria and mitochondria.

p53   A tumor-suppressor gene that is mutated in about half of all human cancers. The normal function of the *p53* protein is to block passage through the cell cycle when DNA damage is detected.

parthenogenesis   A natural form of animal cloning whereby an individual is produced without the formation of haploid gametes and the fertilization of an egg.

pathogen   An organism that causes disease.

PCR (polymerase chain reaction)   A method for amplifying specific regions of DNA by temperature cycling a reaction mixture containing the template, a heat-stable DNA polymerase, and replication primers.

peptide bond   The chemical bond that links amino acids together to form a protein.

pH   Measures the acidity of a solution as a negative logarithmic function (p) of H^+ concentration (H). Thus a pH of 2.0 (10^{-2} molar H^+) is acidic, whereas a pH of 8.0 (10^{-8} molar H^+) is basic.

phagocyte   A cell that engulfs other cells or debris by phagocytosis.

phagocytosis   A process whereby cells engulf other cells or organic material by endocytosis. A common practice among protozoans and cells of the vertebrate immune system. (Derived from the Greek word *phagein,* "to eat.")

phenotype   Physical characteristics of a cell or organism.

phospholipid   The kind of lipid molecule used to construct cell membranes. Composed of a hydrophilic head-group, phosphate, glycerol, and two hydrophobic fatty acid tails.

phosphorylation   A chemical reaction in which a phosphate is covalently bonded to another molecule.

photoreceptor   A molecule or cell that responds to light.

photosynthesis   A biochemical process in which plants, algae, and certain bacteria use energy obtained from sunlight to synthesize macromolecules from CO_2 and H_2O.

phylogeny   The evolutionary history of an organism, or group of organisms, often represented diagrammatically as a phylogenetic tree.

pinocytosis   A form of endocytosis whereby fluid is brought into the cell from the environment.

placebo   An inactive substance that looks the same, and is administered in the same way, as a drug in a clinical trial.

plasmid   A minichromosome, often carrying antibiotic-resistant genes, that occurs naturally among prokaryotes. Used extensively as a DNA cloning vector.

platelet   A cell fragment, derived from megakaryocytes and lacking a nucleus, that is present in the bloodstream and is involved in blood coagulation.

ploidy   The total number of chromosomes (n) that a cell has. Ploidy is also measured as the amount of DNA (C) in a given cell relative to a haploid nucleus of the same organism. Most organisms are diploid, having two sets of chromosomes, one from each parent, but there is great variation among plants and animals. The silk gland of the moth *Bombyx mori*, for example, has cells that are extremely polyploid, reaching values of 100,000C. Flowers are often highly polyploid, and vertebrate hepatocytes may be 16C.

point mutation   A change in DNA, particularly in a region containing a gene, that alters a single nucleotide.

polyploid   Possessing more than two sets of homologous chromosomes.

portal system   A system of liver vessels that carries liver enzymes directly to the digestive tract.

probe   Usually a fragment of a cloned DNA molecule that is labeled with a radioisotope or fluorescent dye and used to detect specific DNA or RNA molecules on Southern or northern blots.

promoter   A DNA sequence to which RNA polymerase binds to initiate gene transcription.

prophase   The first stage of mitosis. The chromosomes are duplicated and beginning to condense but are attached to the spindle.

protein   A major constituent of cells and organisms. Proteins, made by linking amino acids together, are used for structural purposes and regulate many biochemical reactions in their alternative role as enzymes. Proteins range in size from just a few amino acids to more than 200.

protein glycosylation   The addition of sugar molecules to a protein.

proto-oncogene   A normal gene that can be converted to a cancer-causing gene (oncogene) by a point mutation or through inappropriate expression.

protozoa   Free-living, single-cell eukaryotes that feed on bacteria and other microorganisms. Common examples are *Paramecium* and *Amoeba*. Parasitic forms are also known that inhabit the digestive and urogenital tract of many animals, including humans.

purine A nitrogen-containing compound that is found in RNA and DNA. Two examples are adenine and guanine.

pyrimidine A nitrogen-containing compound found in RNA and DNA. Examples are cytosine, thymine, and uracil (RNA only).

radioactive isotope An atom with an unstable nucleus that emits radiation as it decays.

randomized clinical trial A study in which the participants are assigned by chance to separate groups that compare different treatments; neither the researchers nor the participants can choose which group. Using chance to assign people to groups means that the groups will be similar and that the treatments they receive can be compared objectively. At the time of the trial, it is not known which treatment is best.

reagent A chemical solution designed for a specific biochemical or histochemical procedure.

recombinant DNA A DNA molecule that has been formed by joining two or more fragments from different sources.

regulatory sequence A DNA sequence to which proteins bind that regulate the assembly of the transcriptional machinery.

replication bubble Local dissociation of the DNA double helix in preparation for replication. Each bubble contains two replication forks.

replication fork The Y-shaped region of a replicating chromosome. Associated with replication bubbles.

replication origin (origin of replication, ORI) The location at which DNA replication begins.

respiratory chain (electron transport chain) A collection of iron- and copper-containing proteins, located in the inner mitochondrion membrane, that utilize the energy of electrons traveling down the chain to synthesize ATP.

restriction enzyme An enzyme that cuts DNA at specific sites.

restriction map The size and number of DNA fragments obtained after digesting with one or more restriction enzymes.

retrovirus A virus that converts its RNA genome to DNA once it has infected a cell.

reverse transcriptase An RNA-dependent DNA polymerase. This enzyme synthesizes DNA by using RNA as a template, the reverse of the usual flow of genetic information from DNA to RNA.

ribosomal RNA (rRNA) RNA that is part of the ribosome and serves both a structural and functional role, possibly by catalyzing some of the steps involved in protein synthesis.

ribosome A complex of protein and RNA that catalyzes the synthesis of proteins.

rough endoplasmic reticulum (rough ER) Endoplasmic reticulum that has ribosomes bound to its outer surface.

Saccharomyces Genus of budding yeast that are frequently used in the study of eukaryote cell biology.

sarcoma Cancer of connective tissue.

Schwann cell Glia cell that produces myelin in the peripheral nervous system.

screening Checking for disease when there are no symptoms.

senescence Physical and biochemical changes that occur in cells and organisms with age.

signal transduction A process by which a signal is relayed to the interior of a cell where it elicits a response at the cytoplasmic or nuclear level.

smooth muscle cell Muscles lining the intestinal tract and arteries. Lacks the striations typical of cardiac and skeletal muscle, giving it a smooth appearance when viewed under a microscope.

somatic cell Any cell in a plant or animal except those that produce gametes (germ cells or germ cell precursors).

somatic cell nuclear transfer Animal cloning technique whereby a somatic cell nucleus is transferred to an enucleated oocyte. Synonomous with cell nuclear replacement.

Southern blotting The transfer of DNA fragments from an agarose gel to a piece of nylon filter paper. Specific fragments are identified by hybridizing the filter to a labeled probe. Invented by the Scottish scientist E. M. Southern in 1975.

stem cell Pluripotent progenitor cell, found in embryos and various parts of the body, that can differentiate into a wide variety of cell types.

steroid A hydrophobic molecule with a characteristic four-ringed structure. Sex hormones, such as estrogen and testosterone, are steroids.

structural gene   A gene that codes for a protein or an RNA. Distinguished from regions of the DNA that are involved in regulating gene expression but are noncoding.

synapse   A neural communication junction between an axon and a dendrite. Signal transmission occurs when neurotransmitters, released into the junction by the axon of one neuron, stimulate receptors on the dendrite of a second neuron.

syncytium   A large multinucleated cell. Skeletal muscle cells are syncytiums produced by the fusion of many myoblasts.

syngeneic transplants   A patient receives tissue or an organ from an identical twin.

tamoxifen   A drug that is used to treat breast cancer. Tamoxifen blocks the effects of the hormone estrogen in the body. It belongs to the family of drugs called antiestrogens.

T cell (T lymphocyte)   A white blood cell involved in activating and coordinating the immune response.

telomere   The end of a chromosome. Replaced by the enzyme telomerase with each round of cell division to prevent shortening of the chromosomes.

telophase   The final stage of mitosis in which the chromosomes decondense and the nuclear envelope reforms.

template   A single strand of DNA or RNA whose sequence serves as a guide for the synthesis of a complementary, or daughter, strand.

therapeutic cloning   The cloning of a human embryo for the purpose of harvesting the inner cell mass (ES cells).

topoisomerase   An enzyme that makes reversible cuts in DNA to relieve strain or to undo knots.

transcription   The copying of a DNA sequence into RNA, catalyzed by RNA polymerase.

transcriptional factor   A general term referring to a wide assortment of proteins needed to initiate or regulate transcription.

transfection   Introduction of a foreign gene into a eukaryote cell.

transfer RNA (tRNA)   A collection of small RNA molecules that transfer an amino acid to a growing polypeptide chain on a ribosome. There is a separate tRNA for amino acid.

transgenic organism   A plant or animal that has been transfected with a foreign gene.

trans-Golgi network   The membrane surfaces where glycoproteins and glycolipids exit the Golgi complex in transport vesicles.

translation   A ribosome-catalyzed process whereby the nucleotide sequence of an mRNA is used as a template to direct the synthesis of a protein.

transposable element (transposon)   A segment of DNA that can move from one region of a genome to another.

ultrasound (ultrasonography)   A procedure in which high-energy sound waves (ultrasound) are bounced off internal tissues or organs producing echoes that are used to form a picture of body tissues (a sonogram).

umbilical cord blood stem cells   Stem cells, produced by a human fetus and the placenta, that are found in the blood that passes from the placenta to the fetus.

vector   A virus or plasmid used to carry a DNA fragment into a bacterial cell (for cloning) or into a eukaryote to produce a transgenic organism.

vesicle   A membrane-bounded bubble found in eukaryote cells. Vesicles carry material from the ER to the Golgi and from the Golgi to the cell membrane.

virus   A particle containing an RNA or DNA genome surrounded by a protein coat. Viruses are cellular parasites that cause many diseases.

western blotting   The transfer of protein from a polyacrylamide gel to a piece of nylon filter paper. Specific proteins are detected with labeled antibodies. The name was inspired by the original blotting technique invented by E. M. Southern.

yeast   Common term for unicellular eukaryotes that are used to brew beer and make bread. Bakers yeast, *Saccharomyces cerevisiae,* is also widely used in studies on cell biology.

zygote   A diploid cell produced by the fusion of a sperm and egg.

FURTHER READING

꘠

Alberts, Bruce. *Essential Cell Biology.* New York: Garland Publishing, 1998.

Clinicaltrials.gov. "Gene Therapy Clinical Trials." Available online. URL: http://clinicaltrials.gov/search/term=gene%2Btherapy. Accessed October 21, 2003.

Cystic Fibrosis.com. "Gene Therapy for Cystic Fibrosis." Available online. URL: http://www.cysticfibrosis.com/genomics.html. Accessed October 21, 2003.

Genetics and Public Policy Center. "The Regulatory Environment for Human Gene Therapy." April 2003. Available online. URL: http://www.dnapolicy.org/policy/humanGeneTransfer.jhtml. Accessed October 21, 2003.

Genetic Science Learning Center. "Human Genetics." Available online. URL: http://gslc.genetics.utah.edu. Accessed October 21, 2003.

The Globe and Mail. "Couple Can't Grow Baby to Provide Blood." December 20, 2002. Available online. URL: http://www.theglobeandmail.com/servlet/ArticleNews/front/RTGAM/20021220/wbaby1220. Accessed October 21, 2003.

IMB Jena (Institute for Molecular Biology). "Molecules of life." Available online. URL: http://www.imb-jena.de/IMAGE.html. Accessed October 21, 2003.

Krstic, R. V. *Illustrated Encyclopedia of Human Histology.* New York: Springer-Verlag, 1984.

Lentz, Thomas L. *Cell Fine Structure: An Atlas of Drawings of Whole-Cell Structure.* Philadelphia: Saunders, 1971.

Mader, Sylvia S. *Inquiry into Life.* Boston: McGraw-Hill, 2003.

National Center for Biotechnology Information. "Genes and Disease." Chromosome maps of all genes known to cause human diseases.

Available online. URL: http://www.ncbi.nlm.nih.gov/books/bv.fcgi? call=bv.View..ShowSection&rid=gnd.preface.9. Accessed October 21, 2003.

National Institutes of Health. "Enhancing the Protection of Human Subjects in Gene Transfer Research at the National Institutes of Health." Available online. URL: http://www.nih.gov/about/ director/07122000.html. Accessed October 21, 2003.

National Institutes of Health. "Stem Cell Information." Available online. URL: http://stemcells.nih.gov/index.asp. Accessed October 21, 2003.

National Institutes of Health. "Stem Cells: A Primer." May 2000. Available online. URL: http://www.nih.gov/news/stemcell/primer.html. Accessed October 21, 2003.

Nature. "Double Helix: 50 Years of DNA." Many articles assembled by the journal to commemorate the 50th anniversary of James Watson and Francis Crick's classic paper describing the structure of DNA. Available online. URL: http://www.nature.com/nature/dna50/ index.html.

New York Times. "Bone Marrow Found to Have Cells to Repair the Pancreas." March 15, 2003. Available online. URL: http://www.nytimes. com/2003/03/15/health/15STEM.html. Accessed October 21, 2003.

New York Times. "Politically Correct Stem Cell Is Licensed to Biotech Concern." December 11, 2002. Available online. URL: http://www. nytimes.com/2002/12/11/business/11STEM.html. Accessed October 21, 2003.

New York Times. "U.S. Study Hails Stem Cells' Promise." June 27, 2001. Available online. URL: http://www.nytimes.com/2001/06/27/politics/ 27RESE.html. Accessed October 21, 2003.

Oak Ridge National Laboratory. "Gene Therapy." Available online. URL: http://www.ornl.gov/TechResources/Human_Genome/medicine/ genetherapy.html. Accessed October 21, 2003.

Scientific American. "Bone Marrow Stem Cells Reach Brain and Acclimate." January 22, 2003. Available online. URL: http://www. scientificamerican.com/article.cfm?chanID=sa003&articleID=000 9B400-B9F5-1 E2D-8B3B809EC588EEDF. Accessed October 21, 2003.

Sherman, Silverstein, Kohl, Rose and Podolsky. "The Gelsinger Lawsuit." Available online. URL: http://www.sskrplaw.com/links/health-care2.html. Accessed October 21, 2003.

Sherman, Silverstein, Kohl, Rose and Podolsky. "Gelsinger Settlement Press Release." Available online. URL: http://www.sskrplaw.com/gene/pressrelease.html. Accessed October 21, 2003.

Sherman, Silverstein, Kohl, Rose and Podolsky. "Researcher Wilson to Step Down as IHGT Head." SSKRP Attorneys in the News. April 23, 2002. Available online. URL: http://www.sskrplaw.com/publications/newwilson.html. Accessed October 21, 2003.

University of Leicester. "Virus Families." http://www-micro.msb.le.ac.uk/3035/3035virusfamilies.html. Accessed October 21, 2003.

U.S. Food and Drug Administration. "Cellular and Gene Therapy." Available online. URL: http://www.fda.gov/cber/gene.html. Accessed October 21, 2003.

Washington Post. "Penn Settles Gene Therapy Suit: University Pays Undisclosed Sum to Family of Teen Who Died." November 4, 2000. Available online. URL: http://www.washingtonpost.com/ac2/wp-dyn?pagename=article&node=&contentld=A1 1512-2000Nov3.

WEB SITES

Center for Biologics Evaluation and Research. FDA center responsible for monitoring gene therapy. http://www.fda.gov/cber/about. html. Accessed October 21, 2003.

CNN.com. Contains many links dealing with the stem cell debate. http://www.cnn.com/SPECIALS/2001/stemcell. Accessed October 21, 2003.

Cystic fibrosis. http://www.cysticfibrosis.com. Accessed October 21, 2003.

The Department of Energy Human Genome Project (United States). Covers every aspect of the human genome project, including applications to gene therapy. http://www.ornl.gov/TechResources/Human_Genome. Accessed October 21, 2003.

The Journal of Gene Medicine. Links to gene therapy trials. http://www.wiley.co.uk/genetherapy/clinical. Accessed October 21, 2003.

Gene Therapy Advisory Committee (United Kingdom). http://www.doh.gov.uk/genetics/gtac/index.html. Accessed October 21, 2003.

Gene Therapy Department, University of Southern California. http://www.humangenetherapy.com. Accessed October 21, 2003.

Genetic Science Learning Center at the Eccles Institute of Human Genetics, University of Utah. An excellent resource for beginning students. This site contains information and illustrations covering basic cell biology, animal cloning, gene therapy, and stem cells. http://gslc.genetics.utah.edu. Accessed October 12, 2003.

Human Fertilization and Embryology Authority. http://www.hfea. gov.uk. Accessed October 21, 2003.

Institute of Molecular Biotechnology, Jena, Germany. Image Library of Biological Macromolecules. http://www.imb-jena.de/IMAGE. html. Accessed October 21, 2003.

National Center for Biotechnology Information (NCBI). This site, established by the National Institutes of Health, is an excellent resource for anyone interested in biology. The NCBI provides access to GenBank (DNA sequences), literature databases (Medline and others), molecular databases, and topics dealing with genomic biology. With the literature database, for example, anyone can access Medline's 11,000,000 biomedical journal citations to research biomedical questions. Many of these links provide free access to full-length research papers. http://www.ncbi.nlm.nih.gov. Accessed October 21, 2003.

The National Human Genome Research Institute (United States). The institute supports genetic and genomic research, including the ethical, legal, and social implications of genetics research. http://www.genome.gov. Accessed October 21, 2003.

National Institutes of Health (United States). Links to stem cell articles and a stem cell primer. http://www.ncbi.nlm.nih.gov. Accessed October 21, 2003.

Nature. The journal *Nature* provides a comprehensive guide to the human genome. This site provides links to the definitive historical record for the sequences and analyses of human chromosomes, All papers, which are free for downloading, are based on the final draft produced by the Human Genome Project. http://www.nature. com/nature/focus/humangenome/. Accessed October 21, 2003.

Roslin Institute. The place where Dolly the sheep was cloned. Provides articles and photographs about the cloning of Dolly and other animals. http://www.roslin.ac.uk. Accessed October 21, 2003.

United Kingdom Parliament. House of Lords report on stem cells use and legislation. http://www.parliament.the-stationery-office.co.uk/pa/ld/ldstem.html. Accessed October 21, 2003.

U.S. Food and Drug Administration. Provides extensive coverage of general health issues and regulations. http://www.fda.gov. Accessed October 12, 2003.

The White House. Provides links to policy statements and presidential directives concerning therapeutic cloning. http://www.whitehouse.gov. Accessed October 21, 2003.

INDEX

✖

Italic page numbers indicate illustrations.

A

actin 98
actin filaments *88,* 89
AD. *See* Alzheimer's disease
AD-2. *See* adenovirus type 2
AD3 gene 12
AD4 gene 12
ADA. *See* adenosine deaminase
adaptive immune response *37,* 38
adenine 38, 91, 93
adenosine deaminase (ADA) 38–40
  gene for 3, 32–33, 40
  linking to polyethylene glycol (PEG) 40
adenosine deaminase (ADA) deficiency 3, 32–33, 40

adaptive immune system destroyed by 38
conventional treatment for 3, 33, 40
first gene therapy trial for (DeSilva trial) xvi, 32, 42–43
  proposal for 40–41
  shortcoming of 122
gene therapy for clinical procedure 42
  combining with stem cell therapy 43–44
  preliminary research on 40–42
  success rate of 43–44, 45
adenosine diphosphate (ADP) 91

adenosine monophosphate (AMP) 91
adenosine triphosphate (ATP)
  neuron requirements for 47
  production of 65–67, *66,* 89, 105
  recycling of 38–40, *39*
  structure of 91
adenosine triphosphate (ATP) synthetase 65, 105
adenovirus(es) 17–19
  computerized model of *19*
  diseases caused by 19
  life cycle of *25,* 27
  structure of *15,* 16, *18*
  transmission electron micrograph (TEM) of *20*

adenovirus(es)
(*continued*)
  use in gene
    therapy 29–30,
    46, 50
      ban on 46, 52
adenovirus type 2
  (AD-2), use in gene
  therapy 29–30
ADP. *See* adenosine
  diphosphate
agarose 114
AGC (codon) 103
aggression, gene
  therapy aimed at
  controlling 69
aging, gene therapy
  aimed at reversing
  69
AIDS virus (HIV)
  19–22
  entry into cell 27
  hybrid with Ebola
    virus 31
  infection of hemo-
    philiacs with 9
  structure of *21*
  three-dimensional
    drawing of *22*
alpha-synuclein 13
Alzheimer, Alois 12
Alzheimer's disease
  (AD) 11–12
  gene therapy trials
    for 123–124
  and Parkinson's
    disease 13

amino acids 89
  catabolism of 9
  codons specifying
    103, *104*
  in prebiotic Earth
    environment 48
  and protein
    construction 91,
    103–105
  structure of *90*
ammonia 9–10
  buildup of, effects
    of 46–47
  enzyme that rids
    body of 10, 46
  in prebiotic Earth
    environment 48
  in urea cycle 46, *47*
ammonia intoxication
  48
AMP. *See* adenosine
  monophosphate
amyloids 12
anaphase
  of meiosis I *99*,
    100–101
  of mitosis *97*, 98
Anderson, W. French
  32, 40, 41, 42, 43
  and origins of
    gene therapy 79
antigens 38
  vector 59
apolipoprotein E 10
Archaea 87
arginine
  buildup of 48
  in urea cycle *47*

astronauts, gene
  therapy potential
  for 68
A-succinate, in urea
  cycle *47*
ATG (codon) 105
atherosclerosis
  10–11
ATP. *See* adenosine
  triphosphate
ATP synthetase 65,
  105
autosomal recessive
  genetic defect 33

B

BACs. *See* bacterial
  artificial chromo-
  somes
bacteria
  human genes
    obtained from
    120–121
  origins of 87
  plasmid exchange
    among 23, 108
  restriction
    enzymes isolated
    from 107
bacterial artificial
  chromosomes
  (BACs) 119
bacteriophage G4
  119
bacteriophage
  lambda 111, 119

baldness, treating with gene therapy 69
basophils *36*
Batshaw, Mark 45
  abuses in Gelsinger clinical trial 53–54
  as defendant in civil lawsuit 83
  and OTC deficiency gene therapy trial 46, 52
B cells (B lymphocytes) 2, 36, *36*
  in adaptive immune response 38
  in SCID-X1 122
behavior, gene therapy aimed at controlling 69
Belmont Report 71–74, 86
beneficence, principle of 72–73
bilirubin 51
biologics 80
  regulation of 80, 81
biotechnology. *See* recombinant DNA technology
Blaese, Michael 32, 40, 41, 42, 43
blood clot. *See also* clotting disorder
  formation of 7–8, *8*

bone marrow, lymphocytes developing in 2
bone marrow transplant, for ADA deficiency 3, 33, 40
BRAC1 (breast cancer 1) gene 4
BRAC2 (breast cancer 2) gene 4
brain
  cellular debris in, with Parkinson's disease 12
  lesions in, with Alzheimer's disease 12
breast cancer 4–5
breast cancer cell, scanning electron micrograph (SEM) of *4*

C

CAG-CAG-nucleotide triplet repeat 13
calcium chloride, role in human physiology 65
cancer. *See also* specific types
  causes of 4
  gene therapy trials aimed at curing 1

vector-induced 56–57, 122, 123
Caplan, Arthur 83
capsid, viral 16, 23
  release into cytoplasm 27
capsid protein 27
cardiovascular disease 10–11
catabolism, of amino acids 9
CBER. *See* Center for Biologics Evaluation and Research
CDKN2. *See* cyclin-dependent kinase N2
cDNA. *See* complementary DNA
cDNA library 112
cell(s). *See also* eukaryotes; prokaryotes
  chromosome of, insertion of viral DNA into 57, *58*
  division of 95, *95*, 96
  first living and nitrogen fixation 48
  origins of 23, 87
  of immune system 35–36

cell(s) *(continued)*
improved target-
ing in gene ther-
apy 59–61, *60,*
64
macromolecules of
91–95, *92*
membrane of
23–24, 93
molecules of
89–91, *90*
receptors of 23,
24, 27
study of xi–xii
cell cycle *95,* 95–96
S phase of 101
Center for Biologics
Evaluation and
Research (CBER)
80, *81*
central nervous sys-
tem, vulnerability to
ammonia levels 47
centromere 96
centrosome *88,* 89,
97
ceramide *106*
CF. *See* cystic fibrosis
CFTR gene 7
cheetah 77
cholesterol, buildup
of 10
Christmas, Stephen
9
Christmas disease 9
chromatids. *See* sister
chromatids

chromosomes
duplicated 96, *97*
homologous 100
insertion of viral
DNA into 57, *58*
citrulline
buildup of 48
in urea cycle 46, *47*
clinical trials 34–35
for ADA defi-
ciency xvi, 32,
42–44
for Alzheimer's
disease 123–124
for breast cancer 5
for colon cancer 5
experimental
nature of xvi, 75
failure to report
toxic reactions in
53, 64
first successful xvi
for hemophilia 9
for Huntington's
disease 124
for liver disease
10, 29
number of 43, 45
Phase I 34
Phase II 34–35
Phase III 35
Phase IV 35
regulation and
monitoring of
xv, 80–83, *81*
research preceding
33, 34

risk assessment of
63–65, 73–74
for SCID-X1
56–57, 121–123
Clinton, Bill 74
cloning, of DNA
108–111, *110*
labeling in
112–113
clotting disorder,
OTC gene therapy
trial and 51–52, 53
clotting factor VIII
8–9
sources for
replacement
therapy 9
clotting factor IX 9
codons 103–105, *104*
cold, viruses causing
19
colon cancer 5
coma, with liver dis-
ease 10
combined immunod-
eficiency 32. *See
also* severe com-
bined immunodefi-
ciency syndrome
complementary DNA
(cDNA) 112
contig 119
copper, role in
human physiology
65, 67–68
core (p24) protein
21, *21*

coronary arteries, cardiovascular disease affecting 11
cosmetic gene therapy 69–70
  ethics of 77–78
  National Institutes of Health on 83
Crick, Francis 15
crystals, viruses as 15, 16
cyclin-dependent kinase N2 (CDKN2) 5
cyclosporine 61
cysteine 103
cystic fibrosis (CF) 6–7
cytochrome b 65, 105
cytochrome oxidase 65, 67, 105
cytokines 2
  defective receptors for 3
cytokinesis 98
cytosine 91, 93
cytoskeleton 88, 89

D

dATP. See deoxyadenine triphosphate
Davidson, Beverly 124
dCTP. See deoxycytosine triphosphate

dendritic cells 36
  and adaptive immune response 38
deoxyadenine triphosphate (dATP) 112
deoxycytosine triphosphate (dCTP) 112
deoxyribonucleotides 112
deoxyribose 91
Department of Energy (DOE) 119
DeSilva, Ashi xvi, 32, 42
DeSilva clinical trial xvi, 32, 42–43
  approval of Phase I for 42
  proposal for 40–41
  shortcoming of 122
  success of 43–44, 59
  vector safety confirmation prior to 41
DIC. See disseminated intravascular coagulation
dideoxynucleotides 113
digestive tract, cells of, ATP needed by 47

disaccharides 95
disseminated intravascular coagulation (DIC) 51–52
DMD. See Duchenne muscular dystrophy
DMD gene 11
DNA
  cloning of 108–111, 110
  double helix molecule of 93, 94
  nucleotides of 91, 93
  replication of 101–103, 102, 112
  sequencing of 113–115, 114, 115, 116, 119
  structure of 92
  viral, integration into cellular chromosome 57, 58
DNA ligase 107, 111
DNA-modifying enzymes 107–108
DNA polymerase 101, 102, 112, 113
DNA viruses 16, 17–19
DOE. See Department of Energy
Down's syndrome, and Alzheimer's disease 12

Duchenne muscular dystrophy (DMD) 11
dystrophin 11

E

Ebola-HIV viral hybrid 31
Ebola virus *30*
*Eco*RI 110, 111
elderly, causes of death among 12
electron transport chain (respiratory chain) 65–67, *66*, 89, 105
    gold/silver-based 67–68
EMEA. *See* European Agency for the Evaluation of Medicinal Products
endocytosis, receptor-mediated *24, 27*
endoplasmic reticulum (ER) 87, *88*
enhancers 111
envelope, of retrovirus *21*
    formation of 28
envelope protein 27
env gene 20
eosinophils *36*
ER. *See* endoplasmic reticulum

Escherichia coli 110, 111, 119
ethics of gene therapy 71–78
ethidium bromide 108
eukaryotes
    adaptability of 101
    diploid 98
    gene organization in 121
    genome of 87
    membrane of 14, 24, 63
    mitosis used by 96
    origins of 87, 105
    structural components of 87–89, *88*
European Agency for the Evaluation of Medicinal Products (EMEA) 86
European Union, regulatory agencies in 86
exocytosis 28, 89
exons 121
eye color, controlling with gene therapy 69

F

fat, stored in body 93–94

fatigue, reducing 68
fatty acids, structure of *90, 91*
FDA. *See* Food and Drug Administration
Federal Food, Drug, and Cosmetic Act (1936) 80
fibrin, role in clotting process 8, *8*
fibrinogen, role in clotting process 8, *8*
filter hybridization 115, 116, *117*
FISH. *See* fluorescent in situ hybridization
Fisher, Alain, gene therapy trial for SCIDs 56–57, 121–123
fluorescent in situ hybridization (FISH) 116–118
food, conversion into energy 67, 105
Food and Drug Administration (FDA) 80
    Belmont Report and 74
    fraudulent misrepresentations to 53, 64, 85
    Gene Therapy Patient Tracking System 55

new initiatives to
protect partici-
pants in gene
therapy trials 55,
81
regulation of gene
therapy trials by
xv, 34, 35, 79,
80–82, 83,
122–123

G

G4 bacteriophage
119
gag gene 20, 21
gametes
amount of DNA
in 100
haploid 98
γc gene, mutation in
121–122
gel electrophoresis
108
Gelsinger, Jesse xvi,
46, 51–52
Gelsinger, John 83
Gelsinger, Paul 51,
52, 83, 84–85
Gelsinger clinical
trial 46, 51–52, 59
abuses in 74–75
investigation fol-
lowing 52–54,
63–64, 74
lawsuit following
83–85

lessons learned
from 75–76
new regulations
following 81
gene(s)
human
number of 120
origins of
120–121
mutation of 1
overlapping 20
gene libraries
111–112
gene therapy. *See also*
clinical trials; vec-
tors
bizarre 70
combining with
stem cell therapy
43–44, 122
cosmetic 69–70,
76, 83
ethics of 77–78
definition of xv
diseases treatable
with xv, 1
ethics of 71–78
experimental
nature of xvi, 75,
86
failure of xvi,
51–52, 54, 56
future prospects
for 56–70
immune rejection
of vector in,
reducing 61–63

legislation and
regulation of
79–86
low efficiency of
61
number of disor-
ders treated with
xvi
physiological
65–69
ethics of
76–77
promise of xvii,
45
risks of xvi, 56,
70, 76–77, 78
safer vehicles for,
need for 56–61
success of xvi, 3,
43–44, 56
targeting of cells
and organs in,
improving
59–61, *60,* 64
Gene Therapy Advi-
sory Committee
(GTAC) 86
genetic code 103,
104
genetic disorders xv
autosomal reces-
sive 33
deaths from 1
genetic diversity,
importance of 77
genomic library
111

Genovo, Inc. 52–53, 75
  as defendant in civil lawsuit 83, 84
germ cells, number of chromosomes in 100
germ line
  ban on gene therapy trials involving 86
  damage/alteration of, gene therapy and risk of 76–77, 78
GH. *See* growth hormone
glucose 89
glycerol 89
  structure of *90*
glycocalyx 23–24, 62–63, 87, 105–107, *106*
  production of 89
glycolipids 87, *106*
glycoprotein(s) 87, *106*
glycoprotein 41 20–21, *21*
glycoprotein 120 20–21, *21*
gold, respiratory chain based on 67–68
Golgi complex 87, *88*
  in cystic fibrosis 7
Golgi vesicles *88*, 89
gp 41 20–21, *21*

gp 120 20–21, *21*
granulocytes 35, *36*
  phagocytosis of invading microbe by 36
growth hormone (GH) gene 69
growth hormone (GH) injections 77
GTAC. *See* Gene Therapy Advisory Committee
guanine 38, 91, 93

H

hair, controlling with gene therapy 69–70
haploid gametes 98
HD. *See* Huntington's disease
heart muscle cells (myocytes) 11
helicase 101, *102*
hemocyanin 68
hemoglobin, substitution of hemocyanin for 68
hemoglobin molecule *2*
  in sickle-cell anemia 1
hemophilia 7–9
hemophilia A 8–9
hemophilia B 9
Henseleit, Kurt 48
herpesvirus, structure of *15*, 16

hierarchical shotgun sequencing 119
Hippocratic oath 72–73
histones 96
HIV. *See* AIDS virus
homologs (homologous chromosomes) 100
hormone receptors, of cell 24, 27
HUGO. *See* Human Genome Organization
human(s), use as experimental subjects, ethical principles for 71–78
Human Genome Organization (HUGO) 119
human genome project 57, 65, 118–121
Huntington's disease (HD) 13
  gene therapy trial for 124
hydrogen ion, binding to NAD 67
hyperammonemic syndrome (hyperammonemia) 48

I

IHGT. *See* Institute for Human Gene Therapy

IL2R. *See* interleukin 2

immune deficiencies 1–3

immune system 1–2
  adaptive response of *37,* 38
  cells of 35–36, *36*
  innate response of 36–38, *37*
  response to gene therapy vector xvi, 59, 61, 64–65

immunity, development of 38

immunizing serum 38

immunodeficiency, combined 32. *See also* severe combined immunodeficiency syndrome

immunosuppresants 61

IND. *See* Investigational New Drug application

independent review committees 74

infectious diseases xv

influenza virus, structure of *15,* 16

informed consent, principle of 73, 74
  failure to adhere to 53, 74, 75, 84

innate immune response 36–38, *37*

inosine 39

Institute for Human Gene Therapy (IHGT), University of Pennsylvania 45, 50, 51

Institutional Biohazard Committee 82

institutional review boards (IRBs) 74, 81

integrase 57, *58*
  designing for sequence-specific vector insertion 59

intelligence, gene therapy aimed at improving 69

interleukin(s), high concentration of 52

interleukin 2 (IL2R) 3

interleukin receptors 121–122

interphase, in cell cycle *95,* 95–96

intervening sequences 111, 121

intestinal cells, ATP needed by 47

introns 111, 112, 121

invertebrates, use of hemocyanin by 68

Investigational New Drug application (IND) 81

ion channels 24–27

IRBs. *See* institutional review boards

iron
  and human skin tone 69
  in respiratory chain 65, 67–68

J

Janus kinase 3 (JAK3) 3

jumping genes 120

justice, principle of 73

K

kinetochore(s) 96, *97*
  in meiosis I 100

Krebs, Hans 48

Krebs cycle *66,* 67, 105

L

labeling, of cloned DNA 112–113

lambda bacteriophage 111, 119

Langerhans cells *36*
  and adaptive immune response 38

LASN virus, as gene therapy vector 42, 43

lawsuits 79, 83–85
legal issues 79–86
leukemia, vector-
  induced 56–57, 122
libraries, gene
  111–112
lipid bilayer
  of cell 14
  of virus 16, 28
liposome 62, 63
liver disease 9–10.
  See also ornithine
  transcarbamylase
  (OTC) deficiency
  gene therapy trials
  for 10, 29
LMO2 gene 56–57,
  122
lungs, in cystic fibro-
  sis 7
lymphocytes 2, 35,
  36. *See also* B cells;
  T cells
  and adaptive
    immune
    response 38
  evaluation of gly-
    cocalyx by 62–63
  as target cells in
    gene therapy 59
lysosomes *88, 89*

M

macrophages 2, 35,
  36
MAO. *See*
  monoamine oxidase

matrix (p17) protein
  21, *21*
maturation promot-
  ing factor (MPF)
  96
meiosis 98–101, *99*
melanoma 5–6, *6*
messenger RNA
  (mRNA) 103
  northern blotting
    performed on
    115–116
  in viruses 20
metals
  role in human
    physiology 65
  skin tone affected
    by 69
metaphase
  of meiosis I *99*
  of mitosis 96, *97*
metaphase plate 96
microbes, invading
  xv
  immune system
    response to 1–2
microtubules *88, 89*
Milstein, Alan 85
mitochondria *88, 89*
  production of ATP
    by 65–67, *66,*
    105
mitosis 96–98, *97*
mitotic spindle 96, *97*
MLH1 gene 5
monera 87
monoamine oxidase
  (MAO) 121

monocytes 35, *36*
  and adaptive
    immune
    response 38
  phagocytosis of
    invading microbe
    by 36
monogenic disorder
  1
monosaccharides 95
motor proteins *97,*
  98
MPF. *See* maturation
  promoting factor
mRNA. *See* messen-
  ger RNA
MSH2 gene 5
multigene therapy
  69
murine leukemia
  virus (MuLV), use
  in gene therapy 29
  in DeSilva trial 42
  in Fischer trial
    56–57
muscle cells, ATP
  needed by 47
muscular dystrophy
  11
mutation, gene 1
myocytes 11
myosin 98

N

NAD. *See* nicoti-
  namide adenine
  dinucleotide

NADH dehydroge-
nase 65, 67, 105
NADH molecule 67
National Institutes of
Health (NIH) 82
ban on AD-vector
gene therapy
trials 46, 52
Belmont Report
and 74
on cosmetic gene
therapy 83
and DeSilva clini-
cal trial 32
funding of clinical
trials by 83
investigation of
Gelsinger clinical
trial by 52–54,
63–64
monitoring of
clinical trials by
xv, 34, 40–41, 79,
80–81, 82–83
new initiatives to
protect partici-
pants in gene
therapy trials
55, 81
and origins of
gene therapy 79
National Research
Act (1975) 72
National Research
Council 119
natural killer (NK)
cells 35–36, 36

in adaptive
immune
response 38
gene therapy vec-
tors destroyed by
61
in SCID-X1 122
Nazi war criminals,
prosecution of 71
Necker Hospital
(Paris, France) 121
NeoR gene 41
nerve growth factor
(NGF) 123
neurological disor-
ders 11–13
neurons, ATP needed
by 47
neutrophils 36
new biology, mean-
ing of term xi
NGF. See nerve
growth factor
nicotinamide ade-
nine dinucleotide
(NAD) 67
NIH. See National
Institutes of Health
nitrogen fixation 48
NK cells. See natural
killer cells
northern blotting
115–116, 117
nucleic acids 91–93
nucleolus 87, 88
nucleotide(s) 91
in amino acids
103–105

decomposition of
38–39, 39
nucleic acids con-
structed from 93
structure of 38, 90
nucleus
of eukaryote 87,
88
lipid bilayer of 14
Nuremberg code of
ethics 71, 86

O

Office of Biotechnol-
ogy Activities
(OBA) 80, 81, 82
Office of Human
Subjects Research
(OHSR) 80, 81
oligo labeling 113
oligosaccharides 95
organ(s), improved
targeting in gene
therapy 59–61, 60,
64
organ transplanta-
tion, gene therapy
compared with 61
ornithine transcar-
bamylase (OTC)
10, 46–47, 47
gene for 49
ornithine transcar-
bamylase (OTC)
deficiency 10, 48
drugs for 45
forms of 49

ornithine transcar-
bamylase (OTC)
deficiency
(continued)
  gene therapy for
    clinical proce-
      dure 49–51
  Gelsinger trial
    46, 51–52, 59
OTC. See ornithine
  transcarbamylase
ovarian cancer 5
oxygen, in respira-
  tory chain 67, 105

P

p16 protein 5–6
p17 protein 21, 21
p24 protein 21, 21
Parkinson, James 12
Parkinson's disease
  12–13
patient advocates 73,
  83
PCR. See polymerase
  chain reaction
PEG-ADA 33, 40
penicillin 71
peptide bonds 91
peroxisomes 88, 89
phagocytic blood
  cells 2
phosphates 89
  structure of 90

phospholipids 62,
  63, 93–94
  structure of 92
physiological gene
  therapy 65–69
  ethics of 76–77
plants
  nitrogen fixation
    by 48
  origins of 87
plasmids 14, 23, 108
  DNA cloning
    using 110–111,
      113
pol gene 20, 21
poliovirus, structure
  of 15, 16
polyacrylamide 114
polyethylene glycol
  (PEG) 40
polygenic disorder 1
polymerase chain
  reaction (PCR)
  118
polysaccharides 95
  structure of 92
potassium chloride,
  role in human
  physiology 65
preclinical research
  33, 34
primase 101, 102
prokaryotes
  gene organization
    in 121
  genome of 87

membrane of 24,
  63
mitochondria
  originating from
    89
nitrogen fixation
  by 48
origins of 87
plasmid exchange
  among 23
protein receptors
  of 23
and respiratory
  chain, origins of
    67
and restriction
  enzymes, origins
  of 108
promoters 111
prophase
  of meiosis I 99,
    100
  of mitosis 96, 97
proteins 91
  construction from
    amino acids 91,
      103–105
  structure of 92
prothrombin, role in
  clotting process 8,
    8
Pseudomonas
  aeruginosa 7
Pure Food and Drug
  Act (1906) 80
purines 38, 91

purine salvage pathway 38
pyrimidine 91

R

RAC. *See* Recombinant DNA Advisory Committee
random primer labeling 113
Raper, Steven 51, 52
  as defendant in civil lawsuit 83
Recombinant DNA Advisory Committee (RAC) 80, *81,* 82, 83
  monitoring of clinical trials by 34
    DeSilva trial 40–41, 42
recombinant DNA technology (biotechnology) 107–118
  birth of xi, xvi
  regulation of 82
regulatory agencies. *See also* specific agencies
  international 86
  in U.S. 80–83, *81*
regulatory protein 27

replication-competent vectors 31, 64
research, preclinical 33, 34
research subjects, selection of 74
respiratory chain (electron transport chain) 65–67, *66,* 89, 105
  gold/silver-based 67–68
restriction enzyme(s) 107–108
  *Eco*RI 110, 111
retroviral integration sites (RISs) 123
retroviral-mediated gene transfer 42
retrovirus(es) 19–22
  hybrid, genetic engineering of 31
  life cycle of *26,* 27–28
  structure of *21*
  use in gene therapy 30–31, 42, 122
reverse transcriptase 19, 112
ribose 89–91
ribosomal RNA (rRNA) 103
ribosomes *88, 89,* 103
  molecule model of *93*

risk assessment 63–65, 73–74
RISs. *See* retroviral integration sites
RNA. *See also* messenger RNA; ribosomal RNA
  nucleotides of 91, 93
  structure of *92*
RNA interference 124
RNA polymerase 103
RNA viruses 16, 19–22
rRNA. *See* ribosomal RNA

S

salts, role in human physiology 65
Sanger, Fred 113, 119
Sanger sequencing reaction 113–114
SCID-X1. *See* severe combined immunodeficiency-X1
serine 103
severe combined immunodeficiency-X1 (SCID-X1) 3, 32. *See also* adenosine deaminase (ADA) deficiency

severe combined immunodeficiency-X1 *(continued)*
cause of 32–33
clinical trials attempting to cure 56–57, 121–123
research on 40–42
sex-change operations 77
sickle-cell anemia 1
silver, respiratory chain based on 67–68
sister chromatids 96
in meiosis I *99*
in mitosis *97, 98*
skin cancer. *See* melanoma
skin tone, controlling with gene therapy 69
sodium chloride, role in human physiology 65
sodium chloride transporter, gene coding for 7
somatic cell(s), amount of DNA in 100
somatic cell mosaicism 10
Southern, E. M. 115

Southern blotting 115
spindle apparatus *88, 89, 96*
mitotic 96, *97*
spinocerebellar ataxia 124
stem cell therapy, combining gene therapy with 43–44, 122
stopping rules, in Gelsinger clinical trial 50–51
failure to adhere to 75
sugar receptors, of cell 24, 27
sugars 89–91
structure of *90*
syphilis, Tuskegee study of 71–72

T

tacrolimus 61
T cells (T lymphocytes) 2, 35–36, *36*
in ADA gene therapy 42
in adaptive immune response 38
defective 3
in SCID-X1 122

telophase
of meiosis I *99*
of mitosis *97, 98*
TGA (codon) 105
TGC (codon) 103
thrombin, role in clotting process 8, *8*
thymine 91, 93
thymus, lymphocytes developing in 2
titer
dosage issues 53–54
three-tiered evaluation protocol for 64
toxic reactions, failure to report 53, 64
transcription 103, *104*
transgenic stem cells, use in gene therapy 43–44
Tuskegee, Alabama, study 71–72, 73
apology to participants in 74
Tuszynski, Mark 123

U

United Kingdom, regulatory agencies in 86
University of California, San Diego 123

University of Iowa 124

University of Pennsylvania
  as defendant in civil lawsuit 83–85
  Institute for Human Gene Therapy (IHGT) 45, 50, 51

uracil 91, 93

urea 10, 46, 49

urea cycle 46, 47, 48
  genetic defects affecting 48, 49
  origins of 49

V

vectors, in gene therapy
  camouflaging of 62–63
  cancers induced by 56–57, 122, 123
  with cell-specific envelope proteins 60, 60–61
  dosage issues regarding 53–54, 64
  immune rejection of, reducing 61–63

immune system's response to xvi, 59, 61, 64–65
  insertional mutagenesis caused by 123
  lipid 62, 62–63
  preliminary trials to confirm safety of 41
  replication-competent 31, 64
  safety issues regarding 56–61
  sequence-specific insertion of 57–59, 64
  viruses as xvi, 14, 28–29

vesicle, formation of 27

Victoria (queen of Great Britain, empress of India) 9

viruses. See also specific types
  cancer caused by 4
  as cellular parasites 23
  diseases caused by 14
  DNA of, integration into cellular

chromosome 57, 58
  entry into cell, strategies for 23, 24, 27
  evolution from bacterial plasmids 23
  genomes of 16–22, 17
  nonrandom insertion of 57
  structure of 15, 15–16
  used in gene therapy 29–31
  as vectors in gene therapy xvi, 14, 28–29

W

Watson, James 15–16

white blood cells 1–2, 35, 36

Wilson, Jim
  abuses in Gelsinger clinical trial 53–54
  as defendant in civil lawsuit 83, 84
  financial interests of 75

Wilson, Jim
  (*continued*)
  and Genovo
    52–53
  and OTC
    deficiency gene
    therapy trial 46,
    50
  position at
    University of
    Pennsylvania 45,
    85

reporting of
  Gelsinger's death
  by 52
Working Group
  on Human Gene
  Therapy 82

X

X-linked severe
  combined
  immunodeficiency

(SCID-X1). *See*
severe combined
immunodeficiency-
X1

.